CLERKS OF THE CLOSET

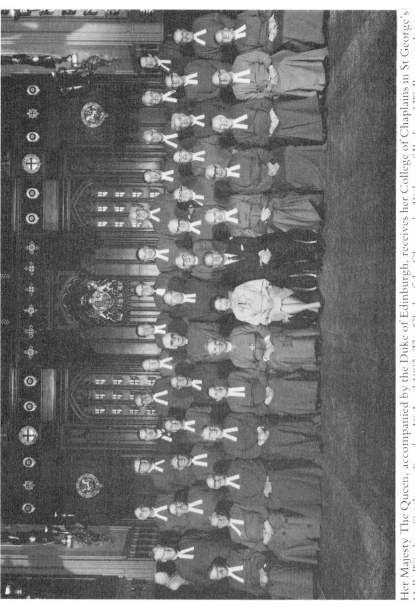

Her Majesty The Queen, accompanied by the Duke of Edinburgh, receives her College of Chaplains in St George's Hall, Windsor Castle, on Sunday 10 April 1983. The Clerk of the Closet, the Bishop of Bath and Wells, seated next to Her Majesty, has Canon Anthony Caesar, L.V.O., F.R.C.O., on his right, and beyond him is Canon James Mansel, K.C.V.O., Deputy Clerk 1965–1979.

Photograph by Kingsley-Jones Studio, Windsor.

CLERKS OF THE CLOSET

IN THE ROYAL HOUSEHOLD

*Five Hundred Years of Service
to the Crown*

*John Bickersteth, sometime Bishop of Bath and Wells
and Clerk of the Closet to The Queen*

*Robert W. Dunning, Editor, Victoria History of
Somerset*

ALAN SUTTON

First published in the United Kingdom in 1991 by
Alan Sutton Publishing Ltd · Phoenix Mill · Far Thrupp · Stroud ·
Gloucestershire

First published in the United States of America in 1991 by
Alan Sutton Publishing Inc · Wolfeboro Falls · NH 03896–0848

British Library Cataloguing in Publication Data
Bickersteth, John *1921–*
   Clerks of the Closet of the Royal Household.
   1. England. Royal households, history
   I. Title II. Dunning, R.W. (Robert William) *1938–*
   354.4203120922

   ISBN 0–86299–873–5

Library of Congress Cataloguing in Publication Data applied for

Typeset in 11/12 pt Bembo.
Typesetting and origination by
Alan Sutton Publishing Limited.
Printed in Great Britain.

Dedicated with gracious permission
to
HER MAJESTY THE QUEEN

CONTENTS

ABBREVIATIONS

Cal. Pat.	*Calendar of Patent Rolls*
Cal. S.P. Dom.	*Calendar of State Papers, Domestic*
D.N.B.	*Dictionary of National Biography*
Hist. MSS. Com.	Historical Manuscripts Commission
LP	*Letters and Papers Foreign and Domestic, Henry VIII*
London Gaz.	*London Gazette*
P.R.O.	Public Record Office

PREFACE

*By the Earl of Airlie, KT, GCVO, Lord Chamberlain of
The Queen's Household.*

WITHIN THE ROYAL Household the Ecclesiastical Household has for centuries held a prominent position. This is indeed to be expected, given the Sovereign's role as Supreme Governor of the Church of England. Its influence has fluctuated over the years but its basic structure has not changed very much. Many of its posts are of great antiquity and amongst them the appointment of the Clerk of the Closet dates back at least to the fifteenth century. Originally the postholder was a minor cleric, but in the course of time he became involved with the personal spiritual life of the monarch. This involvement has varied in importance depending on the religious climate and problems of the day, and probably during the reign of Charles I the Clerk took over the role previously played by the personal Confessor to the Sovereign. Consequently, the history of the post and its holders gives a fascinating and valuable insight into one aspect of the relationship between the monarchy and the church and into the personalities involved.

What is especially striking about the more than fifty holders of the Clerkship since its fifteenth century origin is the great variety of characters involved. Not surprisingly, they include some very distinguished churchmen, including four who went on to become Archbishops of Canterbury and four who became Archbishops of York; but there were also men who were noted as scholars and authors, teachers, literary critics, musicians and scientists.

At least since the sixteenth century the Clerk of the Closet has come under the oversight of the Lord Chamberlain. It therefore gives me great pleasure to congratulate John Bickersteth, Clerk of the Closet from 1979 to 1989, and his co-author, Robert Dunning, on writing this admirable history of a venerable part of the Royal Household.

INTRODUCTION

D URING THE EARLY part of 1980 the news began to filter round the
diocese of Bath and Wells that their Bishop had been made Clerk
of the Closet to The Queen. Comments naturally ranged from the
ribald to the incredulous. 'Is there really such a post?' was a common
reaction as people reached for their copies of Gilbert and Sullivan.

One resident in that same see, who had heard of the office before but
knew almost nothing about it, thought that some research might be
interesting and even useful. But of course the undertaking would have to
be a joint one, and the Bishop found he had little time to spare; for there are
330 parishes to keep a Bishop of Bath and Wells busy, let alone the extra
diocesan work at home and abroad in which everyone in episcopal orders
gets involved.

But as the Clerk's duties started to unfold, and as friendships within the
Royal Household began to develop, the challenge to tell the story of the
office-holders through half a millennium would not go away. There would
obviously be no grand canvas to paint, for the extent of the responsibilities
was not large enough; but worthwhile vignettes would certainly be
possible when previous Clerks were of the calibre of Joseph Butler and
Randall Davidson. Meanwhile, the unrelenting pressures of a diary often
mortgaged months, and sometimes a couple of years, ahead; of thirty to
forty letters a day to deal with; of 250 clergy to care for; 'travels oft' in
Somerset and round the globe – all these continued inexorably and happily
until 30 October 1987, the date chosen for retirement from the see.

Next morning's modest pile of mail in a new home brought the
reminder from the other partner in this enterprise: 'How about that book
on the Clerks, now that you have some time?' Within a month we had
received The Queen's warm encouragement to tackle a study which, so far
as we could tell, had never been done before. One of us was already
familiar with the Public Record Office, the other soon found himself at
home there, a particular delight for him since the bust of his forebear Henry
Bickersteth, Lord Langdale, Master of the Rolls 1836–51 and the PRO's
founder, faces visitors in the entrance hall.

There were two basic questions in our minds: how has the office of Clerk of the Closet developed in the 550 years of its existence, depending so much on the personal relationship of the holder with the Sovereign; and under what circumstances and for what personal or political reasons has the Sovereign chosen men to serve in it? They are, of course, ideal questions; and clear answers have often been difficult, if not impossible, to find. Indeed, it is probable that we have not yet even discovered the names of all the Clerks who have served since the first named one in 1437. This book is, nevertheless, an attempt to compile biographical sketches of the men who have served their Sovereign in this ancient office.

We have, as all authors do, incurred many debts: first to Lord Moore and Sir William Heseltine, the two successive Private Secretaries to Her Majesty and in consequence the Keepers of The Queen's Archives; to the staff of the Royal Library and Archives at Windsor Castle, and especially to Lady de Bellaigue and Mr Oliver Everett; to the staff of Oxford County Record Office; to Miss Margaret Condon of the Public Record Office; to the Revd Dr Nicholas Cranfield, who gave us vital references to Richard Steward and Gilbert Sheldon; to Mr David Herbert, who lent us a remarkably informative personal memoir compiled by his father, Bishop Percy Herbert; to Dr F. W. Dillistone, formerly Dean of Liverpool, who has sent us a valuable pen-picture of Gordon Fallows, Bishop of Sheffield; to Bishop Simon Phipps, who wrote to us about Bishop Roger Wilson, and to Mr David Baldwin, Sergeant of the Vestry, for information from the records of the Chapel Royal. The SPCK generously gave a grant towards research expenses. Much of the important information on the Clerks comes from the official records of the Lord Chamberlain now deposited in the Public Record Office; and the Lord Chamberlain's office has been extremely helpful throughout in providing more modern information. We are most grateful to the Lord Chamberlain, the Earl of Airlie, for kindly agreeing to write a Preface. Our thanks go, too, to our wives, Rosemary and Anne, for meals and coffee at our joint working sessions and for bearing with late-night wrestling with pen or word-processor.

It is our hope that this small book, throwing light on an ancient and still surviving office in the Royal Household, will be an acceptable contribution to a larger and much-needed history of those men and women who have surrounded our Sovereigns and who have together played such an important part in the history of our nation and government.

CHAPTER ONE

IN THE BEGINNING

A FTER THE DEATH of King Henry I in 1135 a statement was made of
the allowances in cash and in food received by members of the
Household of the late King. The document in which this information is preserved, known to historians as the *Constitutio Domus Regis*, the
Establishment of the King's Household, describes the status and activities
of the officials surrounding the sovereign in the earlier part of the twelfth
century.[1]

This is, of course, not the earliest information available about the people
around the sovereign: bishops, lay nobles and clerks are frequently found
witnessing the formal acts of the Saxon Kings, and it is clear enough that
the Saxon royal chaplains, acting as secretaries at need, were the body from
which the formal writing office of the royal government, led by the King's
Chancellor, developed.

So in Henry I's time the Chancellor and his 'department' in the
Household, recorded first in the *Constitutio*, are clearly of the first
importance. The Chancellors themselves – Geoffrey Rufus, Bishop of
Durham, in 1123, Roger le Poer 1135–9 – were not the prominent figures
their successors became, but they were the established heads of the royal
secretariat. In 1135 the Chancellor was sufficiently important to stand at
the head of the Household and to have an allowance of five shillings a day,
one superior and two salt simnels, a sextary (probably four gallons) of
dessert wine and a sextary of ordinary wine, a large wax candle and forty
candle-ends. Next in order in his department came the Master of the
Writing Office, followed by a chaplain to keep the Chapel and the relics,
awarded double rations, and four Sergeants of the Chapel, also with
double rations. Two horses, for which an allowance was given of a penny a
day each for food and a penny a month for shoeing, were the means by
which the Chapel furniture and vestments were moved from place to place
as the sovereign travelled around his realm.

There is in the *Constitutio* nothing about the actual services in the Chapel
Royal, not yet anything about the chaplains, but an allowance was made

for the Chapel of two candles every Sunday and Wednesday, a candle to burn every night before the relics, and thirty candle-ends to light the Chapel itself. A gallon of sweet wine was allowed for the mass, ordinary wine was issued for washing the altar on Holy Thursday, the day of Absolution, and on Easter Day at communion four gallons of dessert wine and one of dry.[2]

The political difficulties of the reign of Edward II gave rise in 1318 to the publication of Household Ordinances which, incidentally, described a much more complicated establishment than that of Henry I. The Chancellor was, by this time, no longer a member of the Royal Household in a practical sense, and the Ordinances began by defining the allowances of the Steward and other officers of the King's Wardrobe, the supply department of the administration.

After the Wardrobe came three senior clerics, the Confessor, the Chief Chaplain and the Almoner. The Chief Chaplain had on his staff an esquire, five chaplains and six clerks, and although there is no direct reference to the King's Chapel, there is no doubt of its existence. Edward II's Chief Chaplain is the Dean of the Chapel Royal of the fifteenth and later centuries, and among the chaplains and clerks are, perhaps, the precursors of the Clerk of the Closet and the Sergeant of the Vestry.

Five years after these Ordinances, others were issued at York which included arrangements for offerings to be made on behalf of the King at the shrine of St Thomas of Canterbury and in the Chapel Royal, and also offerings under the direction of a chaplain for gifts when sufferers came to be healed of the King's Evil.[3]

The Royal Household in the fifteenth century is much less of a mystery, for there survive Ordinances of 1454 and 1478, and several examples of the annual accounts produced by the Wardrobe department of the Household in which are recorded the issue of robes, wine and wages for every member of the royal establishment. The Patent Rolls, the enrolled copies of government correspondence, frequently refer to the Deans of the Chapel Royal or 'deans of the king's chapel in the household', and also to chaplains there, often in relation to their appointment to a Crown living.

The career of Edmund Lacy illustrates very well the personal nature of the post of Dean at the time, and the steps by which a man might first advance within the royal service and then achieve the highest rank outside it. A Doctor in Theology and Master of University College, Oxford, by 1398, Lacy entered the Household in or before 1400 and was rewarded with a canonry in St George's Chapel, Windsor, a royal gift, in 1401. As Dean of the Chapel Royal he accompanied Henry V on the Agincourt campaign in 1415, and went with him as far as Southampton on the next expedition to France in the summer of 1417. But earlier in that year he had been appointed Bishop of Hereford and was consecrated, as was fitting for a royal servant, in St George's. The Chapel Royal and its equipment presumably went with the King across the Channel; Lacy had by that time ceased to be Dean and devoted himself to his new charge, first the diocese of Hereford and then the much larger task as Bishop of Exeter.[4]

The Chapel Royal in the fifteenth century became a vital part of the Royal Household, and the personal interests and inclinations of Henry V, Henry VI and Edward IV are reflected clearly in its development. When Henry V wanted his Chapel with him in France on his second expedition, three men were charged with the oversight and organisation. John Colles, one of the chaplains and described as Servant (or Sergeant) of the Vestry, together first with John Water and later also with John Kyngman, were ordered to arrange for the ornaments, jewels, books, vessels 'and other gear' to be carried by horse and cart to Southampton.[5] Once established in Normandy the King ordered another of the chaplains, John Pyamour, to collect singing boys and take them to the king.[6] Almost a quarter of a century later, the chaplain clearly had responsibility for the singing, too: John Plummer not only looked after the clothing and food of the eight boys of the Chapel, but also taught them.[7] Pyamour and Plummer were among the first in a long line of English composers, known both at home and on the continent, who were employed in the Chapel Royal; a line which included Henry Abyndon and William Newark in the fifteenth century and Thomas Tallis and William Byrd in the sixteenth.[8]

The religious inclinations of Henry VI probably increased the size of the Chapel, and the account of the Keeper of the Wardrobe for the year 1441–2 records the Dean of the Chapel, John Croucher, the Almoner, John de la Bere, and twenty-six chaplains headed by the musician Nicholas Sturgeon. It also includes, near the end of the list, the composer John Plummer, the Sergeant John Midelham and, last but one, a priest named Edward Atherton, elsewhere called Clerk of the Closet. The list seems to have been compiled in order of seniority of entry into the Household, for the same order was regularly kept until at least 1449.[9] The Ordinance of the Household for 1454, however, suggests that the Clerk of the Closet had a higher profile. There he was listed after the Confessor (in Henry VI's time a post of particular influence) and two distinguished chaplains, and before the Chapel Royal and the Vestry.[10]

The Household Ordinances of King Edward IV, issued in 1478, reflect the interests of the King who so magnificently rebuilt St George's Chapel, Windsor, as the centre of a projected Yorkist mausoleum, and was personally concerned with several aspects of the arts. The Chapel Royal figures prominently in the Household, and its members were men of distinction.[11] Magnificence and distinction were both clearly evident at the coronation of Henry VIII and his Queen in June 1509. Present from among the clergy were the Great Almoner, the Under Almoner and the Confessor to the Household; the Dean and Sub-Dean of the King's Chapel; five chaplains and a Gospeller; nineteen gentlemen; the Sergeant of the Vestry and four Epistolers; and ten children. With the Queen came her Confessor, two chaplains and her Clerk of the Closet; and after her procession the pages of the Chamber with the Clerk of the King's Closet and two more chaplains.[12] Small wonder that the Chapel Royal had to suffer with the rest of the Royal Household when the King's financial crisis arose in 1526.[13]

It seems clear, therefore, that within the context of the Chapel Royal, the office of Clerk of the Closet had humble beginnings with the priest Edward Atherton the first actually named as holder of the office. The appointment of Alexander Leigh as Clerk by Edward IV placed a man of learning and political experience in a position of intimacy near the person of the sovereign. Humble functionary had very soon become, and for very many years was to remain, royal counsellor and trusted friend.

NOTES

1. Johnson, C. (ed.), *Dialogus de Scaccario* (Nelson's Medieval Classics, 1950), 129.
2. Chrimes, S.B., *Administrative History of Medieval England* (Blackwell, 1952), 12, 22.
3. Tout, T.F., *The Place of the Reign of Edward II in English History* (Manchester, 1914), 227–9, 317.
4. Emden, A.B., *Biographical Register of the University of Oxford to 1500.*
5. *Cal(endar of) Pat(ent Rolls)*, 1416–22, 127, 132.
6. Ibid., 272.
7. Ibid., 1441–6, 311, 333, 455.
8. Harvey, J.H., *Gothic England* (Batsford, 2nd edn. 1948), 87, 115–16, 124, 142.
9. P(ublic) R(ecord) O(ffice) E 101/409/9, 11; 410/1, 3.
10. Nicolas, N.H. (ed.), *Proceedings and Ordinances of the Privy Council*, vi. 222–3.
11. Myers, A.R., *The Household of Edward IV* (Manchester, 1959).
12. P.R.O., LC 9/50, fos. 207v.–214.
13. *L(etters and) P(apers of) Henry VIII*, iv(1), 862.

CHAPTER TWO

THE CLOSET AND THE 'STUF'

T OWARDS THE END of the Middle Ages, in what is becoming
recognised as the age of private religion, subsidiary chapels of
several different kinds were common in both cathedrals and parish
churches. Private masses for guilds and fraternities, anniversary masses,
chantries and obits were usually established in chapels, each with a separate
dedication and its own ornate and often spectacular design and furnishing.
Some were constructed within the thickness of existing walls and some in
newly-built chapels. Yet others were incorporated within tombs or were
formed by enclosing available spaces with screens. The object was to create
havens for private devotion.

Usually the generic word 'chapel' was applied to these rooms, but in
some places they were known as oratories, as were the chapels in private
houses; and sometimes, as for instance at King's College Chapel, Cambridge, they were called 'closets'.[1] Royal oratories of several kinds were all
known as closets: one was made at Sheen in the 1440s, another within the
chapel at Havering in 1440–41, a third at Ampthill in 1540.[2] Edward IV
planned a closet and altar over his tomb at St George's, Windsor,[3] and in
1505–6 Henry Smyth was paid for metal screens for closets in the Tower
and at Richmond for Henry VII.[4]

The closets in the royal palaces formed part of suites of rooms closely
associated both with the chapels and with the private apartments of the
sovereign. In the 1340s Edward III's private pew or oratory in the Palace of
Westminster seems to have been built on the south side of the altar of
St Stephen's Chapel, allowing him to observe mass privately from an
elevated position, the pew being entered directly from the Painted
Chamber. Close by, perhaps immediately under the pew, was the chapel
of Our Lady of the Pew.[5] Works at Eltham in 1518–28 included the

construction of a floor over the King's pew on the south side of the closet to form a study.[6]

The best detail to survive concerns the closets made for King Henry VIII and Queen Katherine when they attended the Field of Cloth of Gold in 1520. Arrangements were made for the Chapel Royal to be set up at St Nicholas's Church, Guisnes, south of Calais. A gallery was planned to contain the oratory and was to link the church with the royal lodgings at the castle exchequer.[7] From the oratory the King and Queen could look down through windows to the altar on the chapel. The King's oratory, evidently separated from the Queen's by a screen, was hung with cloth of gold and green velvet, and the pew was of the same design, with the King's badge, the rose, and the Garter quartered with lilies. The Queen's pew was in crimson velvet. Each oratory had its own altar, the King's adorned with six statues, a Nativity, St George, St Christopher, St Ursula, St Catherine, and St Barbara. The Queen's altar also had six statues.[8] A similar arrangement was evidently made when Henry VIII met Francis I again at Calais about 1534, when a private closet was made with access to a pew in the gallery of a chapel.[9]

The closets in the two royal chapels of Hampton Court and St James's reveal the same kind of layout. The chapel at Hampton Court was basically Wolsey's work, but it was modified in 1535–6 to provide 'holy-day closets' at the west end for both the King and the Queen, each approached separately by a circular stair or vyce, only one of which still survives. A bay window with the royal arms was built so that the sovereign and his consort could sit in private without being observed by the rest of the Court. The closet at St James's, also at the west end of the chapel, could be reached either from a gallery or up a vyce from the courtyard. Both chapel and closet were built between 1531 and 1541.[10]

New regulations established in 1526 aimed to reduce the cost of the Royal Household by limiting the royal residences where the full staff and liturgy of the Chapel Royal were required. Whenever the King should be at Windsor, Hampton Court, Richmond, Greenwich, Eltham, Woodstock or Bewdley the full staff were to be present; elsewhere, only thirteen choristers and some of the vestry staff were needed.[11] The new palace at Westminster, later known as Whitehall Palace and formerly Wolsey's York Place, became the King's principal residence from 1529. No closet is known to have been made there, but new stalls were built in the chapel quire in 1536.[12] Edward VI lived mostly at Westminster or Greenwich; Queen Mary kept the four chief festivals of the first year of her reign at Westminster, Richmond and St James's, and in her second year one of them at Hampton Court. In 1556 four great turned pillars supporting two carved timbers were erected and painted at the chapel at Hampton Court in association with twenty-four balusters, work which 'may have constituted a screen to the ante chapel or an enclosure for the Queen's pew'.[13]

The use of the word 'pew' implies that the closet was by this time not an oratory with an altar, but rather a place for the sovereign and his or her immediate entourage to sit and hear the liturgy performed. In 1660 the closet at Whitehall chapel had a new wooden screen to afford the King some privacy, although it was well enough known that His Majesty was accustomed to fall asleep until awakened by the Earl of Arlington. Such a screen had not prevented the increasingly loud comments of James I reaching the ears of at least one preacher. In the privacy of the royal pew George I, who understood the English language imperfectly, was wont to talk to the Clerk of the Closet who stood behind his chair and spoke German well. The opening of the chapel in Buckingham Palace in 1843, arising from Queen Victoria's wish not to expose herself and her family to the public gaze on her way to worship in the Chapel Royal at St James's, brought to an end the royal use of that part of the Chapel Royal set aside for the personal and private devotions of the Sovereign, dating back five hundred years.[14]

Gradually, the closet developed from a private chapel or pew and came to be an institution within the Royal Household, financed at first by the Great Wardrobe of the Household of the late medieval kings. In 1509 the Clerk appeared at Henry VIII's coronation with the staff of the King's Chamber.[15] By Elizabeth's reign the Clerk was in the department of the Privy Chamber headed by the Lord Chamberlain, the royal official who continues to deal with the affairs of the Clerk to this day.

'The Stuf of the Closet'

'The Clerk of Closette kepith the stuf of the Closet. He preparith all things for the stuf of the aultrez to be redy, and takyng upp the trauers, leyyng the cuysshyns and carpettes. . . .' So run the regulations set down for the Household of King Edward IV in 1478.[17] The earliest references to the King's Closet are in an account for the years 1427–9, when the young King Henry VI was beginning to attend Mass in private. That account records that a little throne (*parva cathedra*) was upholstered and provided with two long satin cushions.[18] Another account, for the year 1440–41, records that the Clerk of the Closet, by writ and privy bill took delivery from the Great Wardrobe of a hanging valence and a carpet for the Closet. In that same account the Sergeant of the Vestry was credited with various items for the Chapel Royal.[19] Wardrobe inventories of 1492–4 and 1502–3 recorded altars for both the Closet and the Chapel Royal as separate items of responsibility,[20] but thereafter no distinction seems to have been made, and by the time Geoffrey Wrenne handed over his office as Clerk in the 1520s[21] he seems to have been responsible for the ornaments, furnishings and books both of the Closet and the Chapel.[22]

The constant movement of the Court from place to place was clearly more than tiresome for those intimately and practically involved: the Clerk of the Closet received in 1510 some bare hide from the Wardrobe to cover the cart used to transport the Closet 'stuf'; special waggons were needed for the royal Progress to Flanders in 1513, and among the goods belonging to the Chapel Royal in the 1520s were two trussing coffers, a long coffer for tapers and a little one for timber, part of the necessary means by which the Chapel and Closet furnishings were taken from place to place. In 1529 the Privy Purse Office spent cash on a gelding for the Closet and on boat hire for moving 'stuf' from Greenwich to Wolsey's residence, York Place; and at the end of Henry VIII's reign the Clerk signed bills for a pair of trussing coffers delivered to him, together with leather to cover a cart. Small wonder that when new Household regulations were published in 1526 in an attempt to reduce costs, full services were limited to the chapels in seven royal palaces, for it had come to be 'a great annoyance, excessive labour, travail, charge and pain to have the king's whole chapel continually attendant on his person'.[23]

The 'stuf' to be moved was of some variety. When Geoffrey Wrenne took over as Henry VIII's first Clerk in 1509 he received from the Great Wardrobe six altar cloths; in November 1511 he had some sarcenet for mending a traverse; in November 1514 two cloths, one decorated with the figures of the Salutation with a Lilypot on a background of red and white roses. When, some fifteen years later, he handed over his office to Dr Richard Rawson he also handed over at least eleven altar frontals, most of them made of rich arras, two decorated with the Three Kings of Cologne. There were also two hanging tapestries, a pair of linen cloths, some 'sore worn' vestments, cushions and an old carpet. Among the service books were a psalter covered with blue damask with silver clasps, two old Mass books, printed on paper, several other printed books and a manuscript Mass book on vellum 'covered with broken laten'. Among the vast collection of plate which Rawson received from Sir Henry Wyatt, Master of the Jewels, was a golden crucifix with three pointed diamonds, the image of Christ having a ruby in His side, and images of the King's favourite saints: Mary Magdalen, Margaret, Barbara, Peter and Leonard, together with Our Lady and St John the Baptist; and there was a separate jewel of Our Lady and the King himself.[24] The broken laten cover was not the only evidence that the goods and ornaments of the Chapel Royal and the Closet were not in the best condition. William Tebbe, the Sergeant of the Vestry, was sometimes responsible, instead of the Clerk, for restoring vestments as well as providing new ones. In 1530 it was the Clerk who was given £3 11s. to buy six Mass books and velvet to cover them, but three years later the Sergeant took delivery of surplices for the singing men and the children of the Chapel, a set of albs, amices and girdles, eight altar cloths, a little fire shovel, and such practical items as a gallon water pot and two brushes.[25] Thereafter either the Sergeant of the Vestry or an official known as the Keeper of the Closet seems to have been responsible for the practical matters which had once belonged to the Clerk.

Thus, a century after Geoffrey Wrenne took delivery of the stuff, Richard Neile did so formally on taking office in 1608, but two years later the Sergeant of the Vestry, Cuthbert Joyner, was probably in practical control. From 1616 the Sergeant clearly shared his burden, for the pictures and furniture of the Chapel were put in the charge of Inigo Jones in his capacity as Surveyor-General of the Works. In 1631 the repair of the service books was the responsibility either of the Sub-Dean of the Chapel or the Clerk of the Check, and the Dean of the Chapel had general oversight of arrangements when Charles I went to Scotland in 1633, but the Clerk of the Closet paid out money for Closet business during the royal progress in 1638. The Clerk of the Closet was not involved when a warrant was issued for the provision of Prayer Books and a Bible in the Closet for Prince Rupert and the duty chaplains in 1678; and in 1690 it was Gilbert Thornburgh, 'Keeper of the Chapel Closet', who received delivery from the Wardrobe of three dozen large and two dozen small Common Prayer Books, four surplices of fine Holland, two Turkey carpets, three crimson damask cushions, two footstools, four brass plated candlesticks, two strong sumpters and two boxes to put the books in, the whole collection being required for the King's use in the expedition to Ireland.[26] But traditions died hard in the Household, and for long the Clerks retained the ultimate responsibility. In 1756 Bishop Gilbert was required to certify to the Lord Chamberlain that several articles were wanting before John Hart, the 'chapel closet keeper', could take delivery of a total of 147 Prayer Books in various sizes and bindings, four dozen anthem books, a Bible, a trunk for the books, and six Holland surplices.[27] After three centuries the Clerk was still concerned with the 'stuf' of the Closet.

NOTES

1. Colvin, H.M. (ed.), *History of the King's Works*, i. 273–4.
2. Ibid., ii. 959; iv(2), 41.
3. Ibid., ii. 887.
4. B.L. Add. MS. 21480, f. 14v.; Add. MS. 59899, f. 77.
5. *King's Works*, i. 517.
6. Ibid., iv(2), 80.
7. *LP* iii(1), 242.
8. Russell, J.G., *The Field of Cloth of Gold* (1969), 44–5.
9. *King's Works*, iv(2), 14.
10. Ibid., iv(2), 131–2, 134–5, 241; v. 241.
11. *A Collection of Ordinances and Regulations for the Government of the Royal Household* (Society of Antiquaries, 1790), 160–1.

12. *King's Works*, iv(2), 301, 315.
13. P.R.O., E 351/1795; *King's Works*, iv(2), 141.
14. *King's Works*, v. 266; Wraxall, N.W., *Historical Memoirs* (1836), iii. 59; below.
15. P.R.O., LC 9/50, f. 212v.
16. *Collection of Ordinances*, 250–1.
17. Myers, A.R., *The Household of Edward IV* (Manchester, 1959), 137.
18. P.R.O., E 101/408/5.
19. Ibid., E 101/409/6.
20. Ibid., E 101/413/10, 415/10.
21. The exact date has not been traced: see list, appendix 1.
22. See below.
23. *LP* i(1), 301; i(2), 1068; iv(2), 1384; v, 747–8; xxi(2), 404; *A Collection of Ordinances*, 160–1.
24. *LP* i(1), 128, 479; i(2), 1446; iv(2), 1384.
25. Ibid., v, 748; vi, 507.
26. *Cal(endar of) S(tate) P(apers), Dom(estic)* 1603–10, 401, 600; 1611–18, 412; 1631– 3, 94; 1633–4, 18, 31, 33, 38, 47, 68, 153; 1637–8, 173; 1690–1, 18; P.R.O., LC 5/65.
27. P.R.O., LC 5/27, p. 76.

CHAPTER THREE

THE EARLY CLERKS

T HE FIRST REFERENCE to a Clerk of the Closet is quite incidental and is probably a fair reflection of the insignificance of the office at the time. That first holder, Edward Atherton, so far as surviving sources record him, was a long-serving but minor official of the Chapel Royal in the reign of King Henry VI. Under Edward IV, Henry VII and Henry VIII the office still retained its practical functions, but the status of the holder changed radically for two distinct reasons. On the one hand were men of distinction employed on business of national importance: Alexander Leigh served Edward IV as a diplomat, Richard Rawson was a lawyer consulted about Henry VIII's divorce, and Edward Leighton was a theologian involved with the translation of the Bible. On the other hand Peter Greves, Clerk to Henry VII, seems to have been connected with the King on intimate personal grounds, a theme which predominates in the history of the office. The Clerks under the late Tudor Sovereigns were, so far as they can be traced, less distinguished men, under whom the original menial duties probably passed to lesser officials in the Royal Household. Yet the office of Clerk survived partly because it had come to be institutionalised within the very formal organisation of the Court; and also, perhaps, because of the personal influence of the Clerks themselves. Queen Elizabeth's last Clerk, John Thornborough, was the first bishop to hold the office and his political role anticipated the activities of the Clerks under the Stuart Kings.

In March 1437 one of the King's chaplains, EDWARD ATHERTON, on being appointed Warden of the Bethlehem Hospital outside the City of London (the original Bedlam Hospital) was described as Clerk of the Closet.[1] He was sufficiently prominent in the Royal Household to be able to complain two months later that the Hospital was dilapidated, and also in the following year to collect another living in the Crown's gift, the rectory of Diss (Norfolk). He also, for a time, held the rectory of Stamford Rivers (Essex), which he had to resign in 1439.[2] Atherton was listed last but one among the priests of the Chapel Royal in 1441–2, but that may simply have been a reflection of his order of appointment within the chapel and not of the office he held.[3] Certainly, in the Ordinance of the Household of 1454 Atherton was listed after the Confessor and two of the King's chaplains, and before the Chapel Royal and the Vestry. He was named there as 'Sir Edward'.[4] He probably held office until his death early in 1457, when one of those two chaplains succeeded him at Diss and the other at the Hospital.[5]

Two Clerks are known from the reign of Edward IV and they held office together, at least during the year 1466–7. The first was WILLIAM SAVAGE, who had held two livings near Calais between 1462 and 1465, but who has otherwise left no trace so far discovered.[6] The other was ALEXANDER LEIGH, a native of Cumberland, who was educated at Eton and King's College, Cambridge. His career began modestly enough with a chantry at Freckenham (Kent), and it is impossible to say how he entered royal service, possibly through William Gray, Bishop of Ely, who collated him in 1468 to Fen Ditton (Cambs.). His direct rewards from the Crown were canonries of St. George's, Windsor (1469–80) and St Stephen's, Westminster (1476–92). He had presumably ceased to be Clerk by 1474 when he was described as Almoner, and in that year he undertook the first of several diplomatic missions, beginning with the Hanse merchants and travelling to treat four times (once for Henry VII) with the Scots. He was still alive in 1503, four years after suffering a stroke.[7]

Although PETER GREVES was not actually named as Clerk until 1503[8] his appointment to two Crown livings less than a month after Henry Tudor came to the throne is surely a strong suggestion that he was one of that small band of men who had shared the new King's exile.[9] Over the next few years he continued to receive royal patronage, including the church of Diss (Norfolk) which Edward Atherton had once held, and a prebend at St Paul's Cathedral. These rewards and his role as paymaster of several chantry priests saying Masses for the King (see Chapter Ten), suggest that he was Clerk from the beginning of the reign. He attended Henry VII's funeral in 1509,[10] but no further record of his activities has been found.

GEOFFREY WRENNE,[11] Henry VIII's first Clerk, was probably an Oxford graduate. His first living was the vicarage of Brantingham (Yorks.), followed by others in Nottinghamshire and Durham. He was appointed to the living of Warham (Norfolk) by the Crown in 1505, the first of a number of royal gifts which came his way and which included a prebend in York Minster, a canonry at St George's Chapel, Windsor, and the vicarage of New Windsor. The last time he was described as Clerk was in 1514 when he received a cloth livery from the Crown 'at his own proper choice'.[12] Windsor was evidently Wrenne's home, and after his death in 1527 he was buried in St George's Chapel.[13]

His successor, RICHARD RAWSON,[13] was an older man, the son of a

London alderman, and a distinguished lawyer. Probably a Bachelor of Canon Law from Cambridge, he was admitted a Doctor of Civil Law at the University of Bologna in 1489 and a Doctor of Canon Law at Ferrara in 1490. His first known living was a prebend at Salisbury Cathedral, combined, for a short time, with the rectory of Gressenhall (Norfolk) and with the archdeaconry of Essex which he held from 1503 until his death. He was incumbent of several London parishes, for it was in the capital that he was professionally employed, probably as an advocate at Doctors' Commons by 1505,[14] and as a Master in Chancery from 1509. He was present as a royal chaplain at Henry VIII's coronation[15] and held a number of livings in the gift of the Crown including a canonry at St George's, Windsor (1523–43). In 1523 Rawson was one of the lawyers to be consulted about the King's divorce. He left office as Clerk probably in 1529 and died in 1543.

THOMAS WESTBY, Rawson's successor, was also a lawyer, a Bachelor of Canon Law, who was presented to the Crown living of Debden (Essex) in 1528. He was evidently already an established member of the Royal Household, because with three gentlemen of the Privy Chamber he was given the patronage of a prebend at Salisbury Cathedral. In 1533 the Crown presented him to a prebend at Lichfield Cathedral and in June 1540 he became Archdeacon of York. He was dead by 5 January 1544.[16]

Henry VIII's Clerks seem not to have remained in office for long, and Westby was soon succeeded by GEORGE WOLFETT.[17] A native of Durham diocese and a graduate of Oxford and Louvain, he was a Doctor of Canon Law. Rector of St Olave's, Hart Street, London, 1518–28, and vicar of New Windsor 1518–47, he also held a living in Lancashire. Throughout his life he continued to collect benefices as far afield as Durham and Cornwall, and his last appointment was the rectory of Ribchester (Lancs.). He corresponded with Lord Lisle, deputy governor at Calais, on behalf of his servant, and offered Lady Lisle a vestment from the Chapel Royal. He could not, he confessed, spare anything without telling the King except a vestment of new rich tissue 'which serveth for every day'. She actually wanted a tapestry hanging, but all Wolfett could promise was that should her Ladyship's expected child prove to be a boy and the King stood godfather, no doubt he would send it to her. The whole tone of the correspondence suggests a personal intimacy with the King.[18] He died in 1554 and asked to be buried at Ribchester.

EDWARD LEIGHTON or LAUGHTON succeeded Wolfett in 1538. An Oxford theologian, he was the first known Clerk to come from Christ Church (in his time known as Cardinal College and later as King Henry VIII College). He held several university offices and country livings and by 1533 was a royal chaplain. In 1538 he accepted from the Crown the deanery of St Mary's, Stafford and a canonry of Tamworth, and in the following year became Archdeacon of Salisbury. In 1540 he became one of the first prebendaries of Westminster, and in 1548 was appointed vicar of Boughton in Blean (Kent) by Archbishop Cranmer.[19]

From March to May 1540 he was abroad in Calais on a commission of enquiry about possible heresy there, and received 6s. 8d. a day as pay. Two years later he was on a committee of the Lower House of Convocation whose task was to examine corrections made to the Great Bible. During his work on the Bible he and the Dean of Canterbury exhibited at Winchester a version they had made of the Epistle to the Corinthians. From June to August 1544 he was with the King in Boulogne, where he received an allowance of 12d. a day.[20]

JOHN RUDDE, Henry VIII's last Clerk, succeeded Leighton in 1544. He was a Yorkshireman and probably a scholar of Clare College, Cambridge, who later held a fellowship at St John's. Ordained in 1521, he seems to have stayed in Cambridge, where he became Bachelor of Divinity in 1530–31. He was given his first living, the vicarage of Norton (Durham), in 1539.[21] What influence brought him into the Royal Household is unknown, but he signed the claim for expenses in the Closet for the six months from Michaelmas 1544, and in March 1545 he was a witness before the Bishop of London to the confession of Anne Askew. He evidently had influence at Court, for he seems to have procured for a relative the next vacant fellowship at King's Hall, Cambridge. In 1546 he received a pension in respect of a prebend of Burton College which he had just relinquished, and was presented instead to the vicarage of Child Okeford (Dorset). In the same month he was appointed by the Crown to a prebend at St Stephen's, Westminster.[22]

Rudde seems to have served Edward VI as Clerk, and he held prebends at Durham and Winchester cathedrals. As a married priest he would not have been welcome at Queen Mary's Court, and he was deprived of both prebends in 1554, but was soon appointed vicar of Dewsbury (Yorks.). Later he held two other parochial livings in Yorkshire and a prebend at Beverley, married a second time, and died in 1578. He was buried at Durham.[23]

Mary's first Clerk, or at least the first to be traced after Rudde, was JOHN RICARDE, who in May 1554 was given by the Queen the Second Stall at Westminster, clear enough evidence of his close connection with the Royal Household.[24] By Christmas Day 1556, and then described as Clerk of the Closet, he was presented by the Queen to the rectory of St Olave, Southwark, in succession to Owen Oglethorpe, one of Her Majesty's distinguished chaplains, on the latter's promotion to the bishopric of Carlisle. He did not remain in either office for long, for by 10 November 1558 a successor was appointed to St Olave's, vacant by Ricarde's death.

THOMAS THURLANDE was Clerk on Queen Mary's death, and received from the Great Wardrobe the traditional issue of cloth for mourning. A Cambridge graduate, he was appointed to a prebend at Beverley in 1546 and by the Crown to the rectory of All Cannings (Wilts.) in 1554. In 1557 he became vice master of the Savoy Hospital and two years later was elected Master, the first of three successive Masters who were also Clerks of the Closet. Queen Elizabeth did not retain him as Clerk, but he remained a royal chaplain probably until his death in 1574, the Crown adding to his rewards a prebend in Lincoln Cathedral and the rectory of Sparsholt (Hants).[25]

Meanwhile, although most of the personnel of the Chapel Royal including the Dean (George Carew) and the Sub-Dean (Edmund Daniel) and almost all the gentlemen remained in office under the new Queen, a new Almoner was appointed in the person of Dr William Bill, and a new Clerk, WILLIAM YONGE, who was present at the new Queen's coronation. Nothing has been found about his earlier career, and nothing about his activities as Clerk. Described simply as Chaplain in Ordinary, he was presented by the Crown to Stoke Bruerne (Northants) in 1559, and given the eleventh prebend in the newly-founded royal college of St Peter in Westminster in 1560. Yonge was dead by 1579.[26]

Yonge seems to have been succeeded by WILLIAM ABSOLON, possibly a native of Kent, a man who took minor orders in Queen Mary's reign at Wells, where he was usher or under-master at the New School set up by Bishop Gilbert Bourne as a seminary to provide the Church with badly-needed clergy after the wholesale deprivations of married priests. Absolon was made acolyte in September 1556 and three months later a subdeacon, on the title of his prebend in the cathedral which was evidently being used to help finance the school. He proceeded to Corpus Christi College, Oxford, where he later became a fellow. At some unknown date he entered the royal service, for it was as the Queen's Sub-Almoner that he was appointed by Her Majesty to a prebend in Rochester in 1574. Two years later, when he was elected Master of the Savoy, he was described as Chaplain in Ordinary and Keeper of the Privy Oratory (*oratorii secreti*), a unique variation of the older title of Clerk of the Closet. In 1577, like at least one Clerk before him, he was appointed to St Olave's, Southwark.[27]

On New Year's Day 1578, in the normal exchange of gifts between the Sovereign and her subjects, 'Absolon, Master of the Savoy', following George Carew, still Dean of the Chapel Royal, gave to the Queen plate weighing 5 oz and received in exchange a Bible covered with Cloth of Gold, garnished with silver and gilt, and two plates with Her Majesty's Arms. The Queen's gifts were delivered to 'John of the Closet'. In the next year Absolon, this time described as Clerk of the Closet, received another Bible.[28]

Absolon died in 1586, holder since 1579 of the living of Cranfield (Herts.) and since 1581 of Dengie (Essex) as well as the Savoy mastership.

In the last office, as in the office of Clerk of the Closet, he was succeeded by probably the most prominent holder in the later sixteenth century. JOHN THORNBOROUGH was born in Salisbury in 1551. A graduate of Magdalen College, Oxford, he became Bachelor of Divinity in 1582. He was made chaplain to Henry Herbert, Earl of Pembroke, and by him was appointed rector of Orcheston St Mary (Wilts.) in 1575, Marnhull (Dorset) in 1577, and Chilmark (Wilts.) in the same year, that last appointment actually made by the Crown although the patron was the Earl of Pembroke. In the 1580s he was appointed a Chaplain in Ordinary to the Queen, and in 1585 a prebendary of Salisbury.[29]

On New Year's Day 1589 Thornborough, as Clerk of the Closet, presented the Queen with 5¾ oz of plate, receiving in return from Her Majesty's bounty 17¾ oz of gilt plate.[30] In the same year he was appointed Dean of York and continued to hold the deanery until 1617. Meanwhile in September 1593 he was nominated to the bishopric of Limerick, and in the following year he wrote to William Cecil, Lord Burghley, the Lord Treasurer. He had evidently been a member of the Council of the North in York, and now offered his services to the government in Ireland. He proposed to live in Dublin and openly asked permission to take with him animals, muskets and other goods. Less openly ('wrap up my preferred service and duty in silence and oblivion') he suggested he might act as Burghley's agent: 'Yourself should dwell in their bosoms when I dwell in Dublin.'[31] No reply to that letter would have been possible, and whether Thornborough's offer was silently taken up is not known. His appointment first to the see of Bristol (1603–17) and afterwards to that of Worcester (1617–41) suggests that his services were valued. How long he remained Clerk of the Closet is not known: he was still in office on the death of Queen Elizabeth, when he was numbered among the Queen's chaplains, but a cross beside his name in the record of the Queen's funeral suggests that he might not have been present in person.[32]

NOTES

1. *Cal. Pat.* 1436–41, 17.
2. Ibid., 87, 236, 242.
3. P.R.O., E 101/409/9.
4. Nicolas, N.H. (ed.), *Proceedings and Ordinances of the Privy Council*, vi. 222–3.
5. *Cal. Pat.* 1452–61, 336, 338.
6. P.R.O., E 101/412/2, f. 37; *Cal. Pat.* 1461–7, 176, 360, 428.
7. Emden, A.B., *Biographical Register of the University of Oxford to 1500*.
8. P.R.O., LC 2/1, f. 67v.
9. Campbell, W. (ed.), *Materials for the Reign of Henry VII* (Rolls Series), i. 25; *Cal. Pat.* 1485–94, 11, 24.
10. *Cal. Pat.* 1485–94, 255, 303; ibid. 1494–1509, 136, 266; *LP*, i(1), 40–1, 204.

11. Emden, A.B., *Biographical Register*, iii. 2093–4.
12. *LP* i(2), 1446.
13. Emden, A.B., *Biographical Register of the University of Cambridge*.
14. Squibb, G.D., *Doctors' Commons* (Oxford, 1977), 122.
15. P.R.O., LC 2/1, f. 122.
16. *LP* iv(2), 1724, 1897; iv(3), 2488; vi. 141, 280; Le Neve, *Fasti, 1300–1541*, i. 69, vi. 19, x. 36.
17. Emden, A.B., *Biographical Register of the University of Oxford, 1501–40*.
18. *LP* xi(1), 148, 156; xi(2), 22.
19. Emden, A.B., *Biographical Register, 1501–40*.
20. *LP* xv, 170, 229; xvi, 184, 186–7; xvii, 78–9; xix(2), 309.
21. Venn, J. and J.A., *Alumni Cantabrigienses*, iii. 496.
22. *LP* xx(1), 177, 184; xx(2), 550; xxi(1), 67, 778; xxi(2), 74, 83, 99, 404, 443.
23. Venn, J. and J.A., *Alumni Cantabrigienses*, iii. 496.
24. Hennessy, G., *Novum Repertorium Ecclesiasticum Parochiale Londoniense* (1898), 444.
25. Somerville, R., *The Savoy: Manor, Hospital, Chapel* (1960), 238; *Alumni Cantabrigienses*.
26. P.R.O., LC 2/4/2, f. 28v.; LC 2/4/3, p. 108.
27. S(omerset) R(ecord) O(ffice), D/D/Vc 53; *Cal. Pat.* 1572–5, 287; 1575–8, 74; *Somerset Medieval Wills, 1531–58* (Somerset Record Society xxi), 214; *The Registers of Bishops Wolsey, Clerke, Knyght and Bourne* (Somerset Record Society lv), 147; Foster, R., *Alumni Oxonienses, 1500–1714*; Somerville, *The Savoy*, 238.
28. Nicols, J., *The Progresses and Public Processions of Queen Elizabeth* (1823), ii. 77, 88, 260, 271.
29. *Dictionary of National Biography; V.C.H. Wilts.* xiii. 123; Somerville, *The Savoy*, 238–9.
30. Nicols, J., *Progresses and Public Processions of Queen Elizabeth*, iii. 10, 19.
31. Strype, J., *Annals of the Reformation* (1824), iv. 292–3.
32. P.R.O., LC 2/4/4, f. 54.

CHAPTER FOUR

MEN OF FIT WORDS AND HEAVENLY ELOQUENCE

T HE PIETY OF the first two Stuart Kings was of a piece with their view of the sacred, and therefore absolute, power of kingship; and the anti-papist and anti-puritan attitudes of Lancelot Andrewes and William Laud were also found in full measure in the men chosen to serve as Clerks. The post of Confessor to the Household was still part of the establishment of the Chapel Royal,[1] but there is no evidence that the Clerks saw themselves as Confessors, although the intimacy of William Juxon, Matthew Wren and Gilbert Sheldon with Charles I must surely be assumed. So must that between Charles II and both Richard Steward and John Earle, and although that King's conscience was evidently less burdensome to him than those of his father and grandfather, his first two Clerks, Earle and Dolben, were men of proven loyalty to the Church and the Crown. Rather less can be claimed for Blandford, Crew and Sprat, the first perhaps the victim of an academic's miscalculation, the other two as fine examples of self-interest as one could hope to find.

RICHARD NEILE (1562–1640) was educated at Westminster and at St John's College, Cambridge, where he enjoyed the patronage of the Cecil family and was chaplain to Lord Burghley and afterwards to his son, the Earl of Salisbury. He became a DD in 1600 and held the Cecil living of Cheshunt (Herts.). He once preached before Queen Elizabeth, who was 'much taken' with him; and so, too, was James I, who appointed him Clerk in July 1603. On the day Guy Fawkes was arrested Neile was installed as Dean of Westminster, thus increasing his influence at the centre of power. So he could write to Sir Thomas Lake, keeper of the records at Whitehall, with all the confidence of a royal patronage secretary, announcing the death of John Still, Bishop of Bath and Wells, three days earlier, and asking whether the Dean of the Chapel Royal would like the vacant post, and whether if so Sir Thomas's brother Arthur would accept the deanery of Worcester or wait until Winchester should be available. In the event the Dean, James Montague, accepted and Lake went to Worcester.[2] That Neile could write with such freedom about the movement of his senior in the Royal Household speaks eloquently for his influence, and his own subsequent career suggests that his confidence was well placed.

In the summer of 1608 Neile was nominated to the see of Rochester, but he continued to hold the deanery of Westminster until his translation to the see of Coventry and Lichfield in 1610. One of his earliest acts as Bishop was to appoint as his chaplain the young William Laud. To Neile's influence with the King Laud owed his appointment as President of St John's College, Oxford, and also the opportunity to preach for the first time at Court. Neile was promoted to the see of Lincoln in 1614, strongly supported the King in the House of Lords in the same year, and in 1617 attended James on his visit to Scotland. In May 1617 he was nominated to the see of Durham; his energies, and he was now in his mid-fifties, he expended especially on Durham House, in the Strand, where he found room for John Buckeridge and William Laud, by that time Bishop of St David's. The gathering of these and other like-minded men in his London home suggested to some that the house might be better known as Durham College.

Under the new King, Neile was confirmed in his prominent position: in 1627 he became a member of the Privy Council, and was on the commission which exercised the jurisdiction of Archbishop Abbot who was then under suspension. Later in the same year he was elected Bishop of Winchester, and in 1632 Archbishop of York. His uncompromising churchmanship made him prominent in Laud's party, and at Neile's death the Archbishop declared him to have been 'as true to, and as stout for, the Church of England established by law as any man that came to preferment in it'. A competent man of business rather than a scholar, he ordered the northern province with success, but was able to declare that he never deprived any man of his living despite his opposition to the puritan faction.

'The Bishop of Rochester is Clerk of the Closet,' John Chamberlain told Sir Dudley Carleton on 21 June 1617,[3] but Chamberlain was not always well informed nor always able to distinguish fact from court gossip, and it is clear that the man known for telling James I *louche* stories to allay the tedium of court sermons,[4] continued as Clerk until his appointment to York in 1632. In his place Laud secured the appointment of WILLIAM JUXON in order that, as he recorded in his diary,[5] 'I might have one that I might trust near His Majesty if I grow weak or infirm'. Juxon was sworn in on 10 July 1632.

Born in 1582 in Chichester, Juxon went to school in London and in 1598 was elected a scholar of St John's College, Oxford, where he concentrated on the law. He took Holy Orders and became vicar of St Giles, Oxford, where his preaching proved very popular. For six years he lived in a country parish in Oxfordshire until in 1621 he was elected to succeed Laud as President of St John's. Appointed a prebendary of Chichester and a Chaplain in Ordinary to the King, in 1627 he became Dean of Worcester, still retaining the headship of his college and becoming much involved with Laud in the reform of the university.

Juxon resigned from St John's early in 1633, and later in the same year he was elected Bishop of Hereford. Before confirmation, however, Laud secured his appointment as Bishop of London, the new Archbishop wanting a man to succeed him who would, as Clarendon wrote, 'be vigilant to pull up those weeds which the London soil was too apt to nourish'.

Juxon did not hold the Clerkship for long; by August 1633, even before his consecration, he succeeded Laud as Dean of the Chapel Royal, thus forging closer links still with his sovereign. His subsequent career, including the office of Lord High Treasurer 1636–41, exile at Little Compton in Gloucestershire 1649–60, and triumphant if brief return as Archbishop of Canterbury (1660–63) is well known. Perhaps even better remembered is his service to his sovereign in January 1649. After Charles I had been sentenced to death Juxon rarely left his side; he was the only royal servant to attend the King on the scaffold; and was present when the corpse was buried at Windsor in the snow.

On 20 October 1633 Charles I appointed as Clerk a man he had known intimately for eleven years. MATTHEW WREN (1585–1667), who had attracted the attention and support of Lancelot Andrewes and had been entered at Pembroke Hall, Cambridge, where Andrewes was master, was also by his ability in academic dispute noticed by James I. The King appointed Andrewes's chaplain in January 1622 as chaplain to Prince Charles. From that time Wren's rise was secure: he became Master of Peterhouse, Cambridge, in 1625 and his introduction of services in Latin into the chapel which he himself built was a measure of the man and his opinions. In 1628 he was installed Dean of Windsor, and he accompanied the King to Scotland in 1633. In November 1634 he was nominated Bishop of Hereford, but only a little over a year was translated to Norwich: in both sees he made strict enquiry, as Laud clearly wished, into clerical order. In March 1636 Wren was further advanced in the Royal Household when the King appointed him to be Dean of the Chapel Royal.

Wren, who made himself highly unpopular in East Anglia by his measures against the puritans there, was translated to Ely in 1638. In 1641 he was impeached by Parliament and was imprisoned in the Tower, where he remained until 1660, consistently refusing offers of liberty from Cromwell, whose authority he declined to acknowledge. He remained something of an extremist, prepared even to challenge the views of his King. He died in London and is buried in the chapel at Pembroke Hall, Cambridge.

Wren's successor was yet another of those divines of the Laudian school. The exact date of appointment of RICHARD STEWARD has not been found, but it seems likely that when Matthew Wren became Dean of the Chapel Royal in 1636, Steward became Clerk. Steward's career began with much promise and his failure to achieve episcopal office was due entirely to Parliament's ascendancy in religious affairs. The younger son of a Northamptonshire squire, he matriculated at Magdalen Hall, Oxford, in 1609 at the age of fourteen. He took his master's degree in 1615, graduated bachelor of Civil Law two years later, and in 1613 was appointed a fellow of All Souls. For some time he remained at Oxford, but in 1626 was presented by his college to the rectory of Harrietsham (Kent), and was given a prebend at Worcester two years later. In 1629 he moved to Wiltshire where he held the two adjoining livings of Aldbourne and Mildenhall, the one in the gift of the Bishop of Salisbury, the other of the Crown; and in 1630 he was appointed to a prebend at Salisbury. In 1633 he became a Chaplain in Ordinary to the King, and on 6 March 1635 was appointed on Crown nomination Dean of Chichester.[6]

Dr Steward was already Clerk of the Closet when on 20 January a Warrant was issued for £105 in respect of money paid out by him 'for His Majesty's service in the Closet in times of progress'. A letter to him from Dr John Cosin survives, written on 12 March 1638, concerning a sermon preached at Cambridge which advocated confession as necessary to salvation. In the same year he resigned his prebend at Worcester and apparently succeeded Wren as a prebendary of Westminster. On Christmas Eve 1639, unusually for one not of the Foundation, he was appointed Provost of Eton, and in April 1640, as prolocutor of the Lower House of Convocation, he proved invaluable to the King in negotiating subsidies from the Clergy. His reward was appointment to the deanery of St Paul's in 1642 and his (perhaps inevitable) promotion within the Royal Household to be Dean of the Chapel Royal in 1643.[7]

By the end of 1643 this loyal servant of the Crown was under attack. Early in January 1644 a buyer had been found for his confiscated books, and at the end of the month the House of Commons ejected him from the Provostship of Eton. He had by then, in all probability, lost all his other benefices, and appointment to the deanery of Westminster in 1645 was an empty reward. He still, of course, retained the confidence of the King, and in January 1645 vigorously defended episcopacy against the Presbyterians at the Uxbridge Conference. That confidence was soon to be put to a more severe test. In 1646 the King recommended Steward to the Prince of Wales as Dean of his Chapel and one to whom he should defer 'in all things concerning conscience and church affairs'. When next heard of, in 1650, Steward was with his king in Jersey, and he was a regular and respected member of the English Court in exile, accompanying the Duke of York to Paris and Brussels and defending his attendance at Mass. He died in Paris on 14 November 1651, having been visited twice by the King in his last illness, and was buried in the Protestant cemetery at St Germain des Pres.[7]

Anthony Wood described him as 'a noted divine, eloquent preacher, and a person of a smart, fluent stile'; Clarendon called him 'a very honest and learned gentleman, and most conversant in the learning which vindicated the dignity and authority of the Church'. John Evelyn knew him well in exile, and was much affected to find him dead in his lodgings after only two days' illness. 'He was,' he wrote, 'of incomparable parts and great learning, of exemplary life, and a very great loss to the whole church.'[9]

The appointment of the faithful Richard Steward to be the spiritual guide to the Prince of Wales left a gap in the King's Household which GILBERT SHELDON filled with devotion in extraordinary circumstances. The date of his appointment has not been discovered, but Anthony Wood, who owed much to Sheldon's encouragement, declared him to have been Clerk of the Closet,[10] and his closeness to the King from 1646 makes the statement entirely likely.

Sheldon was born in 1598 in Stanton (Staffs.) and was thus only a year or two younger than Steward. He was the youngest son of the bailiff of Gilbert Talbot the great Earl of Shrewsbury, and thus bore his patron's name. He matriculated at Oxford in 1614 and graduated from Trinity College in 1617. He was elected a fellow of All Souls in 1622 and was ordained deacon two years later by the Bishop of Oxford. He was awarded his BD in 1628 and became Doctor of Divinity in 1634. Meanwhile he had found employment as domestic chaplain to Sir Thomas Coventry, from 1625 Lord Keeper of the Great Seal, who, according to Anthony Wood, 'recommended him to King Charles I as a person well vers'd in politics'.[11]

Sheldon was an Oxford man; in 1626 he became Warden of All Souls, and took his turn as Vice-Chancellor of the University. His parochial livings, most under Crown patronage, were modest – with a prebend at Gloucester from 1633, the vicarage of Hackney (Essex) 1633–6, the rectory of Oddington (Oxon.) with Ickford (Bucks.) 1636–9, and the rectory of

Newington (Oxon.) from 1639.[12] His career might have received a setback when he resisted Laud's attempt to appoint Jeremy Taylor to a fellowship of All Souls in 1635 but he was a strong anti-puritan and his friendships with Hyde and Falkland were important. Hyde was later to recall his 'learning, gravity, and prudence [which] raised him to such reputation that he then was looked upon as very equal to any preferment the church could yield'. Hyde also recalled a remark of Sir Francis Wenham that 'Dr Sheldon was born and bred to be archbishop of Canterbury'.

In 1638 Sheldon was appointed Lent Preacher at Court,[13] already a Royal Chaplain with influence. After war broke out he was in frequent attendance on the King, and was present at the Uxbridge Conference with Richard Steward and took a prominent part in the discussions. In 1646 he was with the King at Oxford, the year in which Steward took service with the Prince of Wales. It is likely that Sheldon then succeeded him as Clerk, and it is perhaps to this year that Anthony Wood referred when he declared that the King had designed him to be Master of the Savoy and Dean of Westminster 'that he might the better attend his royal person'.[14] In practice these offices were no longer in the King's gift, but his failure to receive them made no difference to Sheldon's loyalty. The relationship between Sovereign and Clerk was evidently very close, and for thirteen years Sheldon kept secure a paper in which the King vowed to restore church lands and lay impropriations held by the Crown should he be restored to the throne.

Sheldon was with the King in 1647, moving from Royston to be with him at Hatfield, and then for negotiations at Uxbridge. He, Dr Henry Hammond and the Duke of Richmond were identified by Parliament as three who should be removed from the King.[15] At the end of March 1648 Sheldon was ejected from the wardenship of All Souls and had to be removed from his lodgings by force. He was imprisoned in Oxford, but people clamoured to see him in great numbers, to the embarrassment of his captors, and the governor of Wallingford Castle refused to take him. He was freed at the end of the year on his undertaking not to come within five miles of Oxford and not to go to the King in the Isle of Wight. While the King lived, Sheldon acted as 'an important intermediary between Charles and his scattered spiritual advisers' such as Matthew Wren.[16] After the King's death he lived in exile, partly at Staunton Harold (Leics.) with Sir Robert Shirley and 'busied himself raising money for the exiled Court'[17] and for the many dispossessed and penniless clergy in the country.

His reinstatement began early when in 1659 he was quietly restored to the wardenship of All Souls. He met the returning King at Canterbury and was immediately appointed Dean of the Chapel Royal, a fitting post for one who had served his sovereign so loyally and yet who did not hesitate to criticise the conduct of the exiled court. In October 1660 he was elected

Bishop of London in succession to Juxon, and followed him to Canterbury three years later. 'You are the only person about His Majesty that I have confidence in,' Bishop Duppa wrote to him at the Restoration, 'and I persuade myself that as none hath his ear more, so none is likely to prevail on his heart more, and there was never more need of it.' Sheldon's influence remained considerable until his death in 1677, and his generosity, too, was well known. His gifts are thought to have totalled over £72,000 and included, besides the Theatre named after him at Oxford, a contribution to the rebuilding of St Paul's.

On 9 June 1660, only fifteen days after Charles II had been rowed ashore at Dover in the presence of a vast concourse, JOHN EARLE, just made Dean of Westminster, was sworn Clerk of the Closet. There was no doubt who the restored sovereign wished to have at his side after the years of cold and lonely exile – the priest who had been made his tutor so long before, and his close friend for many of those thirty years.

John Earle was the son of the registrar of the Archbishop's Court at York, and was born there about 1601. He matriculated as a commoner at Christ Church, Oxford, in June 1619; but took his degree from Merton a month later. He probably stayed in Oxford as a fellow of Merton for five years, proceeding to MA in 1624, and in 1631 was made Chaplain to Philip Herbert, Earl of Pembroke, Lord Chamberlain of the Royal Household. That post would have given Earle his first lodging at Court, and put him on the road to promotion.

By then he was becoming established as a considerable author. While still a teenager he had published a poem on the death of Francis Beaumont, the dramatist; this was followed by an 'In Memoriam' on the death in action of a soldier (Sir John Burroughs, 1626). Then came *Lines on the return of the Prince from Spain*; after that a Latin poem on the beauty of the Merton garden; and finally his *magnum opus* (1628) which gave him his literary fame: *Microcosmographie, or a Peece of the World discovered in Essayes and Characters*. This work was, after the custom of the time, first published anonymously, but was soon known to be Earle's. It was an instant success, very cleverly drawn 'with much wit and humour' and throwing a great deal of light on the social conditions of the time.

Earle's growing fame as an author acquired for him, according to Clarendon, 'a very general esteem with all men'. He clearly had an attractive and pleasing manner; his conversation was 'so pleasant and delightful, so very innocent, and so very facetious [amusing] that no man's company was more desired or more loved'. The King himself was amused and in 1641 he appointed Earle tutor to his son Charles, so beginning the close association with the future King Charles II. The Oxford don became for more than thirty years more closely attached to Prince Charles's varying fortunes than any other English divine. He remained a staunch loyalist through the mounting tension of the 1640s. To his own great astonishment he was appointed one of the Westminster Assembly of Divines – a remarkable tribute to the high esteem in which he was held across the political divide. He was quite clear, however, that he could not agree to serve on the Assembly, and the combination of his refusal with the fact that he accepted from the Crown the chancellorship of Salisbury Cathedral (he was also vicar of Bishopstone (Wilts.) which was in the royalist Earl of Pembroke's gift) meant that he soon found himself deprived of his livings as a malignant.

During the early part of the Civil War Earle lived in retirement (he was still only in his early forties), but he occupied himself in scholarly pursuits, among them the translation of the whole of Hooker's *Ecclesiastical Polity* into Latin. After the execution of Charles I in 1649 Earle was obviously more than ever concerned for his pupil-become-King who, after defeat at Worcester in September 1651, was a fugitive in his own country for six hunted, penniless weeks until his escape to France – where almost certainly Earle was ahead of his master, as he is said to have been the first to salute the King on his arrival at Rouen.

There, in exile, the scholar-priest and the young King shared in the privations of the Cavaliers' lot, wandering from one debt-haunted corner of the continent to another. 'Every bit of meat, every drop of drink,' wrote the Keeper of the Royal Purse, 'all the fire and all the candles that have been spent since the king's coming hither, is entirely owed for, and how to get credit for a week more is no easy matter.' Through it all Earle moved serenely and peaceably, maintaining his great popularity amid all the squabbling and rancour that were inseparable from high-born men having been thrust into degrading circumstances, begging their bread from contemptuous princes. 'Earle,' wrote Clarendon later, 'was among the few excellent men who never had nor could have an enemy.'

To stand proudly in that late spring of 1660 with the restored King on English soil must have been a supreme and crowning moment for the now ageing and long-loyal cleric. As newly-appointed Dean of Westminster he preached at Court, and assisted at the coronation. He put himself in the forefront of those seeking reconciliation with nonconformist divines, inviting Richard Baxter to preach in the Abbey as clear indication that no bitter feeling was being maintained by the restored Sovereign's loyal servants against any who had become prominent during the Common-wealth period. After Baxter had duly preached in such a royalist stronghold, Earle wrote him a kind and friendly letter, in the margin of which Baxter wrote 'Oh that they were all such'.

Earle was one of the commissioners at the Conference when the Book of Common Prayer was drawn up, and soon after the completion of that task was nominated to the see of Worcester in 1662. He was there less than a year before being translated to Salisbury in 1663. As a member of the House of Lords his conciliatory approach was keenly maintained; he insisted that there was no place for vindictive measures against nonconformists, and spoke out strongly against the first Conventicle Act and the Five Mile Act, both of which were measures designed to limit the activities of nonconformists.

For perhaps six months he was active as Bishop of Salisbury and Clerk of the Closet, but he evidently resigned the Clerkship in the first half of 1664. Eighteen months later he was struck down by a serious illness while with the Court at Oxford, and he died in University College there on 17 November 1665. He lies buried in Merton College chapel, where a highly laudatory Latin inscription was carved on the monument erected to his honour.

'He was a man of all the clergy,' wrote one of his successors, Gilbert Burnet, 'for whom the king had the greatest esteem. He had been his tutor and followed him in all his exile with so clear a character that the king could never see or hear of any one thing amiss in him. So he who had a secret pleasure in finding out anything that lessened a man esteemed for piety, yet had a value for him beyond all the men of his order.'

JOHN DOLBEN (1625–86) was also a House man, having been elected student of Christ Church, Oxford, at the age of fifteen in 1640. From his boyhood Dolben had strong loyalist leanings. He was still only seventeen when he composed a set of Latin iambics to celebrate the return of Charles I from Scotland in 1641; and when, two years later, Oxford became the centre of royalist military operations, he was among the twenty men from his college who became officers in the King's army. Volunteering in time to join the army's march to the north, he rose to the rank of ensign, and while carrying the colours at the battle of Marston Moor (2 July 1644) he was wounded in the shoulder by a musket ball. This, however, did not prevent him from taking an active part in the defence of the city of York, then beleaguered by Fairfax. During the siege he received a severe shot wound in the thigh, the bone was broken, and he was confined to bed for twelve months. As a reward for his bravery he was promoted to the ranks of captain and then major.

By 1646, the year of Dolben's twenty-first birthday, the royalist cause had become hopeless and the army was disbanded, and Dolben went back to his studies. In the following year his courage and loyalty to the Crown came to the fore again when, during the Parliamentary visitation of the University of Oxford he replied to the demand that he should submit to its authority that 'as to his apprehension there was some ambiguity in the words of the question; until it was further explained, he could not make any direct categorical answer to it'. He was at once deprived of his studentship, and his name was removed from the books of the House.

There follows a hiatus of eight years; nothing further is known about him until 1656 when he was ordained by Bishop King of Chichester. Shortly afterwards he married Catherine Sheldon of Stanton (Derbys.), niece of that Dr Sheldon who was to become Archbishop of Canterbury. The Sheldons had a house in St Aldates, Oxford, almost opposite Christ Church, and the Dolbens were able to make their home there for the three remaining years of the Commonwealth. During that time he shared with two others (Dr Fell, the future Dean of Christ Church was one) the honour of privately keeping up the celebration of the sacraments of the proscribed Church of England in defiance of the penal laws. The actual house was opposite Merton, and was the home of Dr Thomas Willis, a well-known Oxford physician whose sister Fell had married. There most of the loyalists of Oxford, especially scholars ejected in 1648, 'did daily resort', so Anthony Wood declared. It is interesting that they seem to have been allowed to do this hard by the colleges they had been forced to leave.

This act of defiance they kept up until the Restoration, and it was hardly surprising that within ten days of Charles II's return two of them should have petitioned the Crown for canonries in their old college. Both petitions were rapidly granted and they returned that same July of 1660 'poor and bare to a college as bare, after the long persecution'. Dolben did his very best to tackle that bareness, contributing generously to the erection of the north side of Tom Quad undertaken by Dr Fell. He was later honoured for that benefaction by having his arms carved on the vault of the great gateway erected by Sir Christopher Wren.

Within little more than two years of the Restoration Dolben acquired a succession of significant livings: in February 1661 the Crown living of Newington-cum-Britwell (Oxfordshire); in April the prebend of Caddington Major in St Paul's Cathedral; in April 1662 the archdeaconry of London and the vicarage of St Giles, Cripplegate; and in December 1662 the deanery of Westminster. The fact that he was married to the niece of the Bishop of London was clearly no hindrance to his promotion, but it was commonly agreed that he was a man of great benevolence, generosity and candour, noted as an excellent preacher, very popular, 'and with other qualities that gave him a mighty advantage of doing much good'.

By 1664 this rising star had become prolocutor of the Lower House of Convocation and the King recognised his loyalty in the same year by appointing him Clerk of the Closet, a position of great difficulty in so licentious a Court. It is to Dr Dolben's credit that, unusually for those days, he gave up his parochial benefices and his archdeaconry shortly after coming to Westminster. There, as Dean, he resolutely maintained the independence of the Abbey from all diocesan control; and soon became one of the most sought-after preachers of his day. His fame was remembered by the poet Dryden in *Absalom and Achitophel* (1681): 'Him of the western dome whose weighty sense flows in fit words and heavenly eloquence'.

The Great Fire of London broke out during his tenure of the deanery, and it is typical of the man that he should have gathered the Westminster scholars in a company, marched at their head to the scene of the conflagration, and kept them at work for many hours, fetching water from the back of St Dunstan's church, which they succeeded in saving.

A bishopric was obviously in store for him, and that winter of the fire he was consecrated in Lambeth Palace Chapel as Bishop of Rochester by the Bishop of London, the sermon being preached by his old friend and fellow-student Dr Robert South. The income of the see was small, so Dolben was allowed to retain the deanery of Westminster, which he did for twenty years. He was spoken of there as 'a very good dean'.

At Rochester he is remembered as a building bishop, and Evelyn's 'most excellent and worthy neighbour',[18] for he tackled the restoration of the severely damaged episcopal palace at Bromley, which had suffered greatly during the Commonwealth. However, he had barely undertaken his new responsibilities before the fall of Clarendon, and he was himself involved in temporary disgrace, being with other bishops forbidden his place at Court. He was then deprived of his Clerkship. So, at any rate, Pepys believed when he recorded a visit to him on 24 February 1667/8 to view an organ at the Deanery. He still lived there 'like a great prelate', the diarist noted, and the disgrace did not last for long. By 1675 he was back in the Royal Household as Almoner, and five years later was nominated to the metropolitan see of York, being enthroned in August 1683 'amidst the universal acclamations of the citizens'.

His short archiepiscopate was one of great vigour. He was said to have been 'much honoured as a preaching bishop, visiting the churches of his diocese and addressing the people in his plain, vigorous style'. He introduced many reforms, not least (and despite the opposition of the residentiary canons) the restoration of the weekly celebration of the Holy Communion which had fallen into disuse. He also, 'with great temper and moderation', strongly urged the keeping of saints' days, defending the institution from the charge of Romish superstition. The best of the clergy and laity declared themselves 'very happy in their archbishop, so active as he was in his station'.

While travelling to York from London in Holy Week 1686 he slept in a room infested with smallpox. He preached in the Minster on Good Friday, but contracted the disease over the Easter weekend and died on Low Sunday at his palace at Bishopthorpe.

Evelyn wrote of the death of the Archbishop 'my special loving friend and excellent neighbour' as an 'inexpressible loss to the whole church, and to his province especially, being a learned, wise, strict and most worthy prelate'. The House of Lords missed him: Sir William Trumbull recorded that 'he was not to be browbeaten there by any courtier or favourite. His presence of mind and readiness of elocution accompanied with good breeding and inimitable wit gave him a greater superiority than any other Lord could pretend to from his dignity of office.' Gilbert Burnet, however, did not entirely like him: 'he was a man of more spirit than discretion, an excellent preacher but of a fine conversation which laid him open to much censure in a vicious court . . . he proved a much better archbishop than bishop', presumably because as archbishop he was resident in his see.

WALTER BLANDFORD, the third Clerk in the Restoration period, also had his undergraduate roots in Christ Church, Oxford, which he entered in 1635 at the age of sixteen. He was admitted a scholar of Wadham three years later, proceeding to a fellowship there in 1644. When the Paliamentary visitors examined the college's senior staff in 1648, he remained in post, presumably because he either took the Covenant or in some way indicated his submission. He was elected Warden of the college in 1659. At the Restoration Blandford, along with hundreds of others in positions of importance in Church and State, was considered sufficiently sympathetic to the royal cause to be appointed chaplain to the Earl of Clarendon, to be given a prebendal stall in Gloucester Cathedral, and to be made Chaplain in Ordinary to the King.

In 1665 he was nominated by the Crown to become bishop of the see he knew so well, Oxford itself. On 7 February 1667 he was sworn in as Clerk of the Closet, but he left office early in 1669, although still only fifty years of age. It is possible that, at a time of immense distrust of the growing influence of Roman Catholics at Court, he lost his position there because of his behaviour at the deathbed of the Duchess of York, the daughter of his friend and patron, the Earl of Clarendon. Blandford naturally went to see her. The Duke of York met the Bishop in the drawing room and told him that his wife had been reconciled to the Roman Catholic church. The Bishop replied that he had no doubt she would 'do well' since 'she was fully convinced and did it not out of any worldly end'. The Bishop then went into the room to see the dying duchess, and made a short Christian exhortation to her 'suited to the condition she was then in'. One does, indeed, wonder how this Church of England bishop put the matter sufficiently delicately! Whether it was an early example of an ecumenical gesture or the misplaced broad-mindedness of an academic, the remark probably cost him the Clerkship.

Blandford remained Bishop of Oxford until 1671, when he was translated to Worcester. He died in 1675.

NATHANIEL CREW (1633–1721) was the son of a peer created by King Charles II a year after the Restoration. The first Baron Crew was a gentleman of considerable fortune who was astute enough to adopt a moderate line of action during the Great Rebellion. Nathaniel, his fifth son, matriculated at Lincoln College, Oxford, in 1653, and soon afterwards became a fellow of the college. The dignity conferred upon his father for the help he gave to the King in promoting the Restoration undoubtedly imbued the young Oxford fellow with a desire for the fruits of royal patronage himself. His own capacity for business was considerable, and by 1668 he had been elected Rector of Lincoln.

Having taken Holy Orders in 1664 he won the favour of the Duke of York, and by his influence he was made Dean of Chichester in 1669. He became Clerk of the Closet in the same year and in May 1671 he was nominated Bishop of Oxford.

Crew now began a discreditable career as the favourite ecclesiastic of the Duke of York, who was in continuing need of a pliant adherent in the Church to connive at his Romish practices. The growing disquiet at the way the House of Stuart was behaving was further reinforced by the marriage of the Duke to Mary of Modena in 1673, in a ceremony performed by Crew. The following year brought him the extra reward of the valuable and prestigious see of Durham, which he was accused of purchasing from Nell Gwynne. In 1675 he baptised the Duke and Duchess's first-born, a daughter, Catherine Laura. He stepped into politics in 1676 by being sworn of the Privy Council.

When Charles II died in 1685 and his brother the Duke of York became James II, Crew continued as Clerk and was very firmly established as sycophant extraordinary to the Crown. 'I could not live if I should lose the king's gracious smiles,' he declared. The Ecclesiastical Commission to which he had been appointed by the Sovereign soon deprived Bishop Compton of London of his spiritual functions; and in 1686 Crew was made Dean of the Chapel Royal and joint administrator of the see of London. His fellow administrator was Thomas Sprat, Bishop of Rochester, who succeeded to the Clerkship of the Closet at the time. Crew and Sprat, together with the Bishop of Peterborough (Thomas White), agreed to draw up a form of thanksgiving when the Queen was again with child, though that was properly the responsibility of the Archbishop of Canterbury. Crew was even prepared to greet the papal nuncio at the King's request, but the coachman refused to drive him for such a purpose. . . !

Yet this unattractive man's career ended much less ignominiously. Realising the consequences to himself of the impending political changes, he did his best to make amends for 'concurring with the Court' for so long. He voted in the House of Lords in favour of the proposition that the throne was vacant because his old master had abdicated, and although excepted by name from the General Pardon of 1690 (he could hardly not be, in view of his well-known behaviour at Court all those years), Archbishop Tillotson magnanimously pressed for Crew's forgiveness. Thereupon he absented himself from London for good, trying to make amends by devoting himself to the pastoral work of a diocesan bishop. In 1697 he succeeded his brother as Baron Crew, the first instance of a peer holding a bishopric.

His generosity in all sorts of good causes soon made him popular in County Durham, and he lived on through two reigns until 1721, when he died at the age of eighty-eight. He bought Bamburgh (Northumb.) from his second wife's family for £20,679, and left this and other property for charitable purposes. There was a large benefaction to his old college, another to found the oration named after him at Oxford; others to small benefices in his diocese to augment their incumbents' income; others again to found charities in various areas of his estates. His Trustees had wide discretionary powers, and in the nineteenth century they largely financed the restoration of Bamburgh Castle.

So Crew enjoys a reputation as a far-seeing philanthropist, and his work in the diocese of Durham over thirty years left a memory of capable and caring administration which to some extent must offset the judgement of such a man as Anthony Wood, who described him as 'a vain Prelate, subservient to the men and religion of those times'.

The last Clerk of the Stuart period was THOMAS SPRAT, in many ways a very distinguished man indeed. He was a native of Dorset, his father having been minister of Beaminster, where Thomas was born, and where he went to 'a little school at the churchyard side'. This must have been a good one, for it enabled him to matriculate from Wadham College, Oxford, in 1651, and to be elected a scholar a year later. He held a fellowship at the college for thirteen years. Wadham was at that time the meeting-place of such men as Seth Ward, Christopher Wren, Ralph Bathurst and others interested in scientific study, and Sprat was drawn into their discussions and pursuits; from these gatherings sprang nothing less than the Royal Society.

Sprat soon began to make himself known by his writings. One piece in particular was to cause him trouble later, a poem written in 1659 *On the death of his late Highness Oliver, Lord Protector*. Twice reprinted and included in the first part of Dryden's *Miscellany*, its adulatory tone frequently exposed him to censure in after years. In fact his name is better known as a versifier than as a master of English prose, which he undoubtedly became.

At the Restoration Sprat's political views changed. He had been ordained priest a month or two before the King's return. In the autumn of 1660 he received a prebend at Lincoln Cathedral which he was to hold for nine years. On the King's visit to Oxford in September 1663 Sprat preached in the university church of St Mary the Virgin, and two days later, when the King visited Sprat's own college of Wadham, he 'spoke a speech'. Sprat also preached before the King on Christmas Eve 1676 at Whitehall, the subject being 'unfeigned simplicity'.

In the early Restoration years, however, Sprat was establishing a formidable literary reputation. A Frenchman, Samuel de Sorbiere, published in 1664 a work entitled *Relation d'un voyage en Angleterre* in which he expanded on the defects of the national character; Sprat, with some assistance from Evelyn, composed a biting reply called *Observations on M. de Sorbiere's Voyage into England*. It was addressed to his friend and frequent correspondent Christopher Wren, and was in fact a popular vindication of Englishmen, adjudged by Addison as 'full of just satire and ingenuity'. Dr Johnson's later comment was that it was 'not ill-performed, but perhaps at least rewarded with its full proportion of praise.'

By now Sprat had been elected a Fellow of the Royal Society and his history of it, published in 1667, was often republished over the next hundred years. In excellent English, it bears out the fact that by now Sprat was widely regarded as a wit and man of letters rather than as a divine and a politician. He was, however, made a canon of Westminster in 1669, given a Lincolnshire living by the Duke of Buckingham in the next year, nominated a chaplain to the King in 1676, and in 1679 made curate and lecturer at St Margaret's, Westminster. That autumn the diarist Evelyn went to St Paul's Cathedral to hear 'that great wit Dr Sprat' and noted that 'his talent was a great memory, never making use of notes, a readiness of expression in a most pure and plain style of words, full of matter, easily delivered'.

So here was a very intelligent Englishman, widely recognised as an attractive preacher, and also a bold upholder of High Church doctrines and of the Divine Right of Kings. A fortunate circumstance procured for him still higher preferment in that he boldly criticised the House of Commons in a sermon before them on 22 December 1680 (they had two sermons on fast days, and this was one of them), implying that they were not as faithful to the King as they should be. This clearly raised his standing at Court and he was made a canon of Windsor; he became Dean of Westminster in 1683, and in the next year Bishop of Rochester. The last two appointments he continued to hold until his death thirty years later.

By the time of his consecration his support for the Crown was further demonstrated by his account of the Rye House Plot against the King in 1683. James II in 1686 invited him to serve on the Ecclesiastical Commission, the device by which James II sought to control the Church for the benefit of his Roman Catholic subjects. Sprat himself perhaps sought to use his position in the hope of gaining the vacant archbishopric of York, but he opposed the Commission's suspension of Bishop Compton. At the end of the year Crew's appointment to succeed Compton as Dean of the Chapel Royal left room for Sprat to be appointed Clerk of the Closet.

In August 1688 Sprat resigned from the Commission because he opposed the prosecution of clergy who refused to read the Declaration against the liberty of conscience, and as Dean of Westminster took his proper place at the coronation of William and Mary. Shortly afterwards he was the victim of a strange conspiracy which alleged that he was plotting for the return of James II. Sprat was arrested in his Palace at Bromley and held for a few days under guard in his Deanery at Westminster. A month later he was released when it was found that the accusations were totally false; but Sprat turned that crisis in his life to good account, putting together an excellent account of the plot against him, subsequently described by Macaulay as one of the best narratives in the language.

After that trauma the bishop, with twenty years of life still ahead of him (and still holding those two major offices, of Westminster and Rochester), passed his days in comparative seclusion. His commission as Clerk was not renewed in 1689, so the Bishop contented himself with repair work at Westminster Abbey under the direction of his old friend Christopher Wren and with building plans at his Palace at Bromley, pulling down and rebuilding the chapel there and much improving the whole building. There he died on 20 May 1713, and was buried on the south side of St Nicholas's Chapel in Westminster Abbey.

A dedicated lover of good living, Sprat thoroughly enjoyed spending money. Lord Ailesbury said of him that 'he was a man of worth, but he loved hospitality beyond his purse.' *Maxime semper valuit auctoritate* runs the inscription on his tomb in the Abbey, and that was a leading trait in his character. Macaulay called him 'a great master of our language'; and Dr Johnson, who was born shortly before Sprat died, had heard it observed 'with great justness' that 'every book by him is of a different kind, and that each has its distinct and characteristical excellence'.

NOTES

The biographies are based on entries in the *Dictionary of National Biography*, and on that of Crew in *Complete Peerage*, iii. 534. Quotations from Evelyn's Diary are from the edition of William Bray (4 volumes, 1887).

1. P.R.O., LC 2/6, f. 42.
2. *Cal. S.P. Dom.* 1603–10, 410.
3. Ibid., 1611–18, 473.
4. Wilson, A., *The History of Great Britain* (London, 1653), 125.
5. Laud, William, *Diary*, in *Works* (Library of Anglo-Catholic Theology, London, 1847–60).
6. *Archaeologia Cantiana* 76 (1961), 164; *V.C.H. Wiltshire*, xii. 83, 137; *Le Neve, Fasti, Salisbury*, 23.
7. *Cal. S.P. Dom.* 1637–8, 173, 305, 365; 1639–40, 175.
8. Matthews, A.G. (ed.), *Walker Revised*, 10; *Le Neve, Fasti, London*, 5–6.
9. Wood, Anthony, *Athenae Oxonienses*, ed. P. Bliss (1813–20) iii. 295; Bray, (ed.), *Evelyn's Diary*, i. 279, 283–4; iv. 135, 243.
10. Wood, *op.cit.*, iv. 854.

11. *Ibid.*; Beddard, R.A., 'Sheldon and Anglican Recovery', *Historical Journal*, xix (1976), 1005–6. We owe this second reference to the Revd Dr Nicholas Cranfield.

12. Hennessy, G., *Novum Repertorium*, 176; *V.C.H. Oxfordshire*, vi. 282.

13. *Cal. S.P. Dom.* 1637–8, 235.

14. Wood, op. cit., iv. 854.

15. *Cal. S.P. Dom.* 1645–7, 564, 593, 597.

16. Beddard, loc. cit., 1008.

17. Jones, J.R. (ed.), *The Restored Monarchy 1660–1688*, (2nd. edn. 1986), 157. We owe this reference to Dr Cranfield.

18. *Evelyn's Diary*, ii. 47.

CHAPTER FIVE

REVEREND, LEARNED AND SOBER

T HE REVOLUTION OF 1688–9 transformed the constitutional position of the Crown in relation to Parliament, but the Sovereign still
remained Supreme Governor of the Church of England and the
fount of ecclesiastical patronage; and Queen Anne retained at least the
outward sign of her family's claim to Divine Right by touching hundreds
of victims of the King's Evil. Several holders of the office of Clerk of the
Closet in the sixty years after the Revolution, and notably Charles
Trimnell and Richard Willis, were outspoken in their support for the
supremacy of Crown over the Church against the high notions of Tory
clergymen. The wise counsels and wide sympathies of Gilbert Burnet and
John Tillotson, Clerks in the early years of William III's reign, proved of
immense importance for both Church and State at a crucial period. Sixty
years later, in the sober years of the Age of Reason, Joseph Butler stood by
his sovereign, a rational man who could not entertain enthusiasm, but who
could speak to that Age in its own language.

To succeed Bishop Sprat at this crucial period the new King, William of
Orange, chose an old and loyal friend, GILBERT BURNET, to be his Clerk of
the Closet. Born into a well-known Aberdeen family (his father Robert
was an advocate), Gilbert was something of an infant prodigy. By the age
of fourteen he had enough Latin and Greek behind him to become Master
of Arts, despite being educated solely by his father until he was ten years
old. He began a study of civil and feudal law when he was fifteen, but
switched next year to divinity as his father was determined that he should
become a clergyman. He is said to have studied for a full fourteen hours a
day! Qualifying within a year as probationer in the Presbyterian church, he
declined a living offered him by a cousin on the grounds that he was not fit

for so important a post when he was still only sixteen years old. It was the first of many signs of grace in this remarkable man.

His father and brother died in the same year, 1661, but though urged by relations to return to his legal studies, a leading Scottish divine named Nairn, who had been a great friend of his father, encouraged him to extend his knowledge of divinity, and it was then that he became imbued with the principles of the 'excellent' Hooker's *Ecclesiastical Polity*, a work which influenced him towards the Church of England. He also then began to practise extempore preaching, which was then most unusual among Scots clergy.

Moving, like other affluent Scots at that time, to the English universities, he met many distinguished literary and academic men. 'I was fortunate,' he wrote later, 'to fall into the hands of such men – they both set me right and kept me right.' Offered the living of Saltoun to encourage his return to Scotland, he chose instead to travel to Holland and France, meeting protestant ministers and establishing in himself, he declared, his love of law and liberty, and his hatred of absolute power. The liberal views he was more and more firmly holding, and the intimacy of his friendship with the Earl of Lauderdale, incurred the jealousy of the Scottish bishops when he returned to England and stayed for some months at Court. He was soon a member of the newly-founded Royal Society, but accepting Saltoun at last devoted himself for a full five years to a most punctilious and imaginative ministry there – overcoming, so his son and biographer declared, the hostility even of the rigid Presbyterians, in spite of the fact that he stood almost alone in making use of Anglican prayers.

Nevertheless, he drew up a memorial during those years against the abuses of bishops, basing his objections to their behaviour on the constitution of the primitive Church, thus hardly endearing himself to them. Yet Robert Leighton, Archbishop of Glasgow, used Burnet to set on foot extensive reforms to reduce the bishops' powers.

It was through Leighton that Burnet was offered the divinity professorship at Glasgow University. He left Saltoun reluctantly, but already on terms of confidence with both the King and the Duke of York, he kept himself well informed on what was happening at Court in both England and Scotland, and from his new position in an important Chair began to be widely consulted on affairs of Church and State. Before long he was offered the choice of four Scottish bishoprics, including Edinburgh, but he declined them all on the grounds that preferment would have limited his growing influence. The King had already made him one of his chaplains, and the Duke of York valued his advice and never-failing self-confidence even more. His former friend the Earl of Lauderdale, however, denounced him to the King; and when Burnet took upon himself the bold task of remonstrating with his Sovereign over his evil life the new chaplain found himself struck off the list for being 'too busy'. The Duke of York effected some kind of reconciliation, but Lauderdale was still active against him and Burnet was shortly afterwards forbidden the Court and ordered to distance himself not less than twenty miles from London. This injunction was not enforced and Burnet, who by now had come permanently to England and was establishing a considerable reputation as a preacher, was able to accept the chaplaincy of the Rolls Chapel, an office which he was to hold for the next ten years.

Only three years passed, however, before the Crown offered him the bishopric of Chichester, perhaps an attempt by the King to be reconciled with this fearless and broad-minded cleric. He seems to have declined the offer, and his denunciations of those in high places continued. In January 1680 he wrote a severe letter to Charles II: 'There is one thing and one thing only which can extricate you from all your troubles. It is not the change of a minister, or of the council, not a new alliance or a session of parliament. It is a change in your own heart and your course of life . . . you have not feared God, but have given yourself up to many sinful pleasures.' Even this powerful rebuke seems to have left his relationship with the King for the most part unaffected, although he was increasingly unpopular with James.

By September 1683 Burnet, who had attended Lord Russell on the scaffold after the Rye House Plot, thought it wise to leave England, and was immediately treated with the highest consideration in France: 'No minister of the King hath had such a reception.' This roused still further the dislike of the Duke of York, and Louis XIV lessened his enthusiasm. Burnet, at some risk, then returned to his native land.

After preaching a vehement sermon on the following 5 November (1684) against popery, Burnet was deprived of his chaplaincy of the Rolls Chapel. On the accession of James II he left England again, this time for Holland, France, Italy, Switzerland and Germany, coming after two years to the Hague, where the Prince and Princess of Orange invited him to live. Thus began the deep friendship between them. The much-travelled, scholarly and yet wordly-wise clergyman was taken totally into the confidence of them both. Burnet urged William to have his fleet in readiness but not to move until the cause was sufficiently important to justify him in all eyes.

The jealousy of King James continued to mount, and he remonstrated twice with William about the position which Burnet occupied in his Court. William diplomatically decided to dismiss him, but he continued to consult him constantly, and both Prince and Princess stood sponsors for his first son by his second wife. The Prince and Burnet did not actually meet again until a few days before William embarked for England, and they landed at

Torbay together in November 1688, the actual place chosen at Burnet's suggestion. The date was 5 November, and when Burnet remarked on the fact the Prince replied: 'Will you not now believe in predestination?' 'I told him,' Burnet recorded, 'that I would never forget that providence of God which had appeared so signally on this occasion.'

Burnet was entrusted with the duty of preventing violence by the Dutch soldiers on the road to Exeter and then London, and when commissioners came from James to treat with William, it was Burnet who urged that the King should be allowed to leave the kingdom unharmed. He was convinced that the Crown should be given to Mary as well as to William, the suggestion which won the day. On 23 December he preached at the Chapel Royal at St James's on the text: 'This is the Lord's doing and it is marvellous in our eyes'; and on 1 February 1689 he was publicly thanked by the House of Commons for a Thanksgiving sermon preached on 31 January.

A Newsletter dated 14 February described the events leading to the offer of the Crown to the Prince and Princess. On accepting, and thus becoming King and Queen, they went from the Banqueting House in Whitehall to the Chapel Royal, where Henry Compton, Bishop of London, preached. Dr Burnet, the Newsletter reported, officiated as Clerk of the Closet to the King, and Dr Stanley to the Queen. He was not to hold the office for long. On 9 March he was nominated Bishop of Salisbury and was consecrated at the end of the same month, having refused the see of Durham on the grounds that its revenues would be heavily charged with the pension of the retiring Bishop, Nathaniel Crew.

Once on the episcopal bench Burnet made immediate and urgent contributions in the House of Lords, for the questions of toleration, comprehension and the oaths of allegiance were of pressing importance, although his influence was probably due more to his position at Court than to his oratory, which seems to have been heavy and rather pedantic. William himself chose Burnet to propose in the House the naming of the Duchess of Hanover and her posterity in the succession of the Crown. When that succession took place in 1701 Burnet was named chairman of the committee to which the bill was referred, and his position at the time marked the beginning of a friendship with the Duchess which lasted until her death.

Burnet preached the coronation sermon in April 1689, and when the King went to Ireland later in that year Burnet was, at the King's express desire, in close attendance on the Queen. During her lifetime she had entire control of church affairs, and on her death such matters were referred to a commission, of which Burnet was a member in 1694 and again in 1700.

On 8 March 1702 Burnet was with Archbishop Tenison at the deathbed of King William; and his most influential work was done. For fifty years he had been the consistent representative of broad church views both in politics and doctrine, and his robust and vivacious nature, his capacity for sustained hard work, and his tolerant and conscientious care for his clergy made him one of the ablest prelates of his day; and a loyal subject of the Prince whom he rightly believed would be the best King of England for those turbulent times.

Burnet's episcopate stands alone as a record of able and conscientious government. He did his best by careful examination to secure a learned and competent clergy, and stood out against admitting unqualified nominees to livings. He waged war against pluralities, and established a divinity school at Salisbury. His famous tolerance both to Nonjurors and to Presbyterians roused the anger of some extremists; and his immense generosity was demonstrated again and again by the way he entertained at his own expense all the clergy summoned to appear at his visitations.

His most lasting achievement, mentioned on his fine memorial in the south aisle of Salisbury Cathedral, was the provision for the augmentation of livings, generally known as Queen Anne's Bounty, an ecclesiastical charity for Church of England clergymen which was to last, under the same name, for nearly 250 years until taken on and administered by the Church Commissioners after the Second World War. What he did was to propose to the King, in two memorials dated January 1696 and December 1697, that the First Fruits and Tenths payable to the Crown but granted away by Charles II to his mistresses and natural children, should be applied to the increase of poor livings. The plan met with sufficient opposition to obstruct it until after King William's death, but Burnet lived to see it become law under Queen Anne in 1704. Burnet's proposals had, curiously enough, an underlying political motive: acceptance of the original plan might secure the support of the clergy in the forthcoming elections. Whatever the motive, generations of Anglican priests were to be grateful for their Queen Anne's Bounty cheque each quarter which alone saved them very often from penury.

At the time James II fled the country JOHN TILLOTSON (1630–94) was rising sixty. He had grown up in turbulent times and had been an undergraduate at Cambridge when Charles I was executed. By 1651 he was a fellow of Clare College, but was not ordained until the year of the Restoration. By then he was thirty and had 'developed a strong appetite for sermons, of which he usually heard four every Sunday and one on Wednesdays'. He was soon to cultivate his own talent as a preacher with extreme care, and once told a fellow priest that he had originally 'written every word of his sermons, and used to get them by heart, but he gave this up because it heated his head so much a day or two before and after he preached'. People who heard him on a Sunday when he was Preacher at

Lincoln's Inn went again on the Tuesday in the hope of hearing the same discourse.

The pulpit had been the great strength of puritanism, but although Tillotson led the way in using it to wean men from those opinions, he retained some of the characteristics of his upbringing. It was said of him at Lincoln's Inn that he gave communion to people sitting, and avoided bowing at the name of Jesus, stepping backwards instead and looking heavenwards, a habit which caused Charles II, who approved of his preaching style, to say that he 'bowed the wrong way, as the Quakers do when they salute their friends'.

Tillotson's most famous sermon was on 'The Wisdom of being Religious', preached in 1664, but his polemical writing against Roman Catholicism began with his 'Rule of Fasting' in 1666, the year he became a royal chaplain.

Though the King disliked his attacks on Popery, he gave Tillotson a prebendal stall at Canterbury in 1670 and made him Dean in 1672. Earlier in that same year (1672) he had preached at Whitehall 'On the hazard of being saved in the Church of Rome', a sermon which caused the Duke of York to cease attending the Chapel Royal.

Tillotson was, indeed, much in favour of concessions to noncon-formists. In 1674 he and Richard Baxter drafted a bill for 'comprehension', whereby those 'formerly ordained by parochial pastors only' were to be authorised to continue within the Anglican ministry by a written agreement which was purposely ambiguous. The negotiation was ended by Tillotson in the following Spring in a letter to Baxter, announcing the hopelessness of obtaining the concurrence of the King or a majority of the bishops. Yet he continued to speak in favour of concessions to noncon-formist scruples.

The puritan judgement on his sermons was that they were 'plain and honest', though some of his expressions were 'dark and doubtful'. The tradition in his home town of Halifax was that his father commented after hearing one of them that he preached well 'but he believed he had done more harm than good'. Much was made of a sermon he preached at Whitehall in 1680 in vindication of the Protestant religion from the charge of 'singularity and novelty'. He had prepared what he had to say at short notice because the appointed preacher was ill. In an unguarded passage he maintained that private liberty of conscience did not extend to making proselytes from 'the established religion'. He did, in fact, mean Protes-tantism by that phrase, but there were complaints in the House of Lords that his words played into the hands of Rome. The point he actually wanted to make was the principle of obedience to constituted authority as providential – in other words, he identified Protestantism with the constitution.

Tillotson preached before William of Orange early in 1689, and proof that he was approved of was his appointment in March as Clerk of the Closet in succession to Burnet. In August of the same year the Canterbury chapter appointed him to exercise the archbishop's jurisdiction because of Sancroft's suspension. In September he was nominated to the deanery of St Paul's, where he was installed in November. On Burnet's advice the King intimated to Tillotson in a private audience that he was to succeed Sancroft at Canterbury, an idea he disliked, for he honestly thought he could do more good where he was. Interestingly, he commented in a paper three years later that there might, perhaps, be as much ambition in declining greatness as in courting it.

Opposition to a bill for comprehension under the Toleration Act was so strong in the House of Commons that Tillotson urged the King to summon Convocation. He was among thirty divines on a commission which prepared for the meeting and which made extensive alterations to the Prayer Book. Pressure continued for him to accept the see of Canterbury, but he remained reluctant, not relishing the idea of being 'a wedge to drive out' Sancroft. He finally accepted nomination in April 1691 and was consecrated a month later. Sancroft still refused to leave Lambeth until he received a writ of ejectment.

Tillotson at once resigned the Clerkship and with his wife Elizabeth set about exercising hospitality at Lambeth. He practised a marked moderation towards both non-jurors and nonconformists. His kindness, good humour and generosity won him high praise. Always a sensitive man, he is reported to have burst into tears over the fury aroused by one of his sermons. He was perhaps the only Primate in a hundred years to take first rank as a preacher: 'Good preaching and good living,' he once commented to a friend, 'will gain upon people.' He regularly gave away a fifth of his income to charity.

His political influence as Archbishop of Canterbury was not significant, but his moderation was of importance in securing the throne for the House of Orange. After his experience on the convocation commission, he preferred to govern the Church by royal injunctions addressed to the bishops. He had a stroke while in the Chapel at Whitehall and died on 22 November 1694. He was buried in the chancel of St Lawrence Jewry, in the City of London, a church with which he had been connected as Tuesday lecturer for thirty years.

Dr THOMAS BURNETT was admitted Clerk of the Closet to His Majesty on 28 November 1691 when he was about fifty-five years old. He was a native of Croft (Yorks.) and attended Northallerton grammar school where he was later held up as a model pupil. He became an undergraduate under Tillotson at Clare College, Cambridge, and in his twenties moved to Christ's, becoming a fellow and later Master there.

In 1685, through the good offices of the Duke of Ormonde, a governor of that ancient foundation, he was made Master of the Charterhouse. King James afterwards wished to appoint a Roman Catholic as a pensioner there, but Burnett led resistance to the appointment and the majority of the governors refused compliance with the King's letters of dispensation. The incident was sufficiently important to be subsequently written up in a pamphlet entitled *Relation of Proceedings at the Charterhouse upon the occasion of King James II presenting a papist*.

Burnett was, however, chiefly known for his 'scientific' writings. He maintained that the earth resembled a gigantic egg; the shell was crushed at the Deluge, the internal waters burst out while the fragments of the shell formed the mountains, and at the same catastrophe 'the equator was diverted from its original coincidence with the ecliptic'. His theories were attacked widely ('I could refute him on a single sheet of paper,' wrote one critic), and Burnett further laid himself wide open to ridicule by giving a ludicrous account of the conversation in Genesis between Eve and the serpent. A popular ballad represented Burnett as saying:

> That all the books of Moses
> Were nothing but supposes . . .
> That as for Father Adam
> And Mrs Eve his madam
> And what the devil spoke, sir,
> Was nothing but a joke, sir
> And well invented flam.

Probably as a result of the inevitable publicity he was forced to give up the Clerkship in 1695. He continued writing to the end of his long life, 'combining an imagination nearly equal to Milton's with solid powers of understanding'. It was said of him during his lifetime that 'though in orders he wore a lay habit'.

The Lord Chamberlain's books record that Dr Thomas Burnett was 'discharged' and that Dr JOHN MONTAGU was appointed Clerk of the Closet on 25 November 1695. Montagu, fourth son of the first Earl of Sandwich, was at Trinity College, Cambridge, as both undergraduate and fellow. Nathaniel Crew was a relative, and it was probably through him that Montagu received a prebendal stall in Durham Cathedral. In the same year, 1683, he was made Master of Trinity, a post he retained until 1699 when he was made Dean of Durham. Presumably he came to royal notice before becoming master, since the appointment was in the gift of the Crown.

Trinity is said to have declined both in numbers and reputation during Montagu's mastership because of the relaxation of discipline which his lazy temper encouraged. But it is known that he was a liberal benefactor to the college, contributing towards the cost of the new library and allowing a sum due to him when he resigned the mastership to be spent on buying furniture for the Master's Lodge.

With his aristocratic background it was, perhaps, natural that he should have been made a member of the Gentlemen's Society in 1723. He died, unmarried, in his London house, Bedford Row, Holborn, on 23 February 1723, and was buried in the family vault at Barnwell (Northants).

On 1 April 1702 JOHN YOUNGER, WILLIAM GRAHAM and SAMUEL PRATT were appointed by Queen Anne 'to remain as our chaplains and to attend as Clerks of our Clossett in their Several waitings', and on 26 November to share the office between them.

Younger entered Christ Church, Oxford, in 1656 but moved to Magdalen and after the Restoration held a fellowship there until 1689. At the same time he was rector of Easton Neston (Northants) (1671–89), Second Keeper of the Bodleian Library, and from 1688 rector and vicar of Bishopstone (Wilts.). He held canonries at Salisbury, Canterbury, and St Paul's. From 1705 until his death in 1728 he was Dean of Salisbury.

A story is told that he was dismissed from Court by Charles, Lord Townshend, one of the Secretaries of State, for persisting in indecorous behaviour in the Chapel Royal. Wraxall, in his *Historical Memoirs*, quoted a story that, anticipating the coming of the Prince of Hanover as King, Younger mastered the German language and was thus continued as Clerk of the Closet. The King frequently conversed with the Clerk during services he could not otherwise understand, and thereby gave great offence. Townshend persuaded the King to cease, but Younger's continued presence tempted him to fall into his old ways. Thereupon Townshend required Younger to withdraw, and the divine, assuming the order to have come from the sovereign, removed himself to Salisbury. Townshend is said to have told the King that Younger's absence was due to his death after a kick from a horse. The dismissal story may, of course, have a grain of truth: the exact date of the appointment of Charles Trimnell has not been found, and Younger may well have stayed in office for the first few months of George I's reign. The King, of course, knew nothing of Townshend's intervention, and some years later, on a visit to Salisbury Plain for a military review, was astonished to find Younger still alive. After mutual explanations the Dean was promised preferment, but his death soon afterwards prevented the King from making a bishop out of his resurrected Clerk.

The second member of Queen Anne's triumvirate was William Graham, of Netherby (Cumberland), yet another Christ Church man. He was appointed a prebendary of Durham in 1684, rector of Whickham (Cumberland) in 1685, and Dean of Carlisle in 1686. He held the deanery until

1704 when he was appointed Dean of Wells, a post he held until his death in 1713. As a dean he would have been a royal chaplain, but he was also Chaplain in Ordinary to Princess Anne and he thus remained in her service when she became Queen.

Samuel Pratt, educated at Merchant Taylors' school from 1666 and at St Catharine's College, Cambridge, was both divine and schoolmaster. He was headmaster of the grammar school at Wye (Kent) and was rector of a country living there between 1682 and 1693. He seems to have moved to London, and in 1697 he was appointed to two royal posts, a canonry of St George's Chapel, Windsor, and the Mastership of the Savoy. He was chaplain and tutor to the Duke of Gloucester (born 1689, died 1700), and also chaplain to Princess Anne. Author of a treatise on the problems of restoring the currency, Pratt was appointed Dean of Rochester in 1706 and died in 1723. He was buried at St George's, Windsor.

Without any question the next Clerk was a man for royalty. CHARLES TRIMNELL (1663–1723) was the eldest of four sons born to the wife of a country parson who held the same living, Abbots Ripton (Hunts.), for forty-six years. The second son became Dean of Winchester, the third Apothecary to the Royal Household, and the fourth Archdeacon of Leicester. The future Clerk of the Closet went to Winchester and New College. During his eight Oxford years he collected four degrees and then, in 1688, became Preacher at the Rolls Chapel, an appointment given him by the Master of the Rolls, Sir John Trevor.

Trimnell was narrowly defeated for the wardenship of New College in 1703, but the next year was presented by the Queen to the rectory of Southmere (Norfolk). Less than four years later, at the age of forty-four, he became Bishop of Norwich.

Trimnell's enthusiasm for the supremacy of the Crown grew with the holding of high office in the Church – when one might have expected the opposite! He maintained that this was the traditional position of the Church, no doubt citing the stand taken by Henry VIII; and in accordance with these views he showed himself strongly opposed to the high church opinions and practices then becoming prominent. In 1709, for instance, he published a charge to his clergy in which, after objecting to 'the independence of the church upon the state', he proceeded to condemn any belief in the power of offering sacrifice or the power of forgiving sins.

As the years passed his position hardened, and he became prominent as a controversialist both in this preaching and in his writing. This in no way deterred the King from making him Clerk of the Closet in 1715, and he was still holding the office at the time of his death on 15 August 1723 at Winchester, to which see he had been translated two years before.

The King's choice of a successor, RICHARD WILLIS (1664–1734), had more than twenty-five years of royal connection behind him, for he had accompanied William III to Holland in 1694 as a chaplain. He had come from humble origins, unusual for a bishop at the time. His father was a journeyman tanner in Worcestershire, but the boy was bright and went to Wadham College, Oxford, from Bewdley Free Grammar school. At the university he was elected a fellow of All Souls in 1688. After ordination he was chosen as Lecturer of St Clement Dane's in the Strand and soon became a well known preacher, with a remarkable capacity for memorising what he had written. He became a prebendary of Westminster in 1695 and in 1699 was one of the original promoters of the Society for Promoting Christian Knowledge.

In 1701 he was made Dean of Lincoln and continued to make a name for himself by his preaching, one of his most elaborate compositions being delivered before Queen Anne on 23 August 1705, the thanksgiving day 'for the late glorious success in forcing the enemy's lines in the Spanish Netherlands by the Duke of Marlborough'.

The new King, George I, made him Bishop of Gloucester three months after his accession, and invited him to preach at Whitehall Palace just after the consecration service. The sermon, entitled 'The Way to Stable and Quiet Times', was delivered before the Court on 20 January, the day of thanksgiving for bringing His Majesty to 'a quiet and peaceable possession of the throne'. It had to be translated into French for the King's benefit.

In 1717 Willis was appointed Almoner in succession to the Bishop of Carlisle. He remained Bishop of Gloucester until November 1721 when he was translated to Salisbury; and less than two years later moved to Winchester. He died suddenly of gout at his London home, Winchester House, Chelsea, on 10 August 1734.

HENRY EGERTON was a member of an aristocratic but not entirely fortunate family. John, Earl of Bridgwater (1646–1701), had six sons, of whom only two survived, and the title became extinct in 1823. Henry, the youngest and second surviving son, matriculated at New College, Oxford, in 1707 at the age of eighteen, and studied civil law, not a usual subject for a cleric. He was appointed to two family livings in Yorkshire, Dunnington and Settrington, in 1713 and to a canonry of Christ Church in 1716. He failed to secure the Deanery of Christ Church in 1719, a fellow canon admitting that 'he would be better . . . than any other that would be likely to be sent'.[1] Two more family livings in Shropshire came in 1720, and in the same year he was recorded as one of the 'under clerks by turns' with Mr Talbot as a deputy to Charles Trimnell, then Clerk of the Closet,[2] probably introduced to Court by his brother Scroop, Lord of the Bedchamber 1719–27. In 1723 he was nominated to the vacant see of Hereford, and it was assumed that he would try to retain his Oxford canonry, for his contemporaries knew him to be a close man. He was consecrated in 1724.

Egerton married Elizabeth Ariana, a daughter of William Bentinck, Earl of Portland. Under her father's will she was to inherit £10,000 from his Dutch estates, or failing them the English ones, but successful claims on the former by her half sisters brought her no more than 50,000 guilders. Egerton, evidently with some reluctance, finally accepted £4,000 on his wife's behalf.[3]

Soon after his arrival in his diocese Egerton made a considerable stir. Dr William Stratford, who had known him when both were canons of Christ Church, told the Earl of Oxford with some relish that he had got himself 'into a fine scrape. . . . He met lately near Whitchurch a loaded cart, the driver of which refused to give way to him: upon this the bishop was dormant in him, and the nobleman alert and predominant. He swore at the carter like a dragoon, and beat and bruised the poor fellow with the butt-end of his whip.' The 'rude rustic' was 'so uncivil as to employ a noted attorney for such matters to take the law of his Lordship.' Egerton apparently offered two guineas by way of compensation, but the lawyer claimed a hundred and hoped for 'lusty damages against one of his character for swearing and striking'. The outcome of the case was not then known (and has not been traced), but Stratford thought that Egerton's love of money was such that he was prepared to risk public exposure in the hope of saving himself some expense.[4]

Three years later Stratford had another story for Lord Oxford. This time both Lady Scudamore and Oxford's son each sent Egerton half a buck on the same day. He kept the fattest and 'sent for his butcher and haggled with him a long time for what he would allow him for Lady Scudamore's ½ buck, and took it out of him in money or meat'.[5]

Little record of his activities as a bishop has survived. Through the Attorney-General in 1745–6 Egerton initiated proceedings against the churchwardens of Whitchurch, Shropshire, for their failure to support their free school;[6] and he demolished an unwanted chapel. He was made Clerk of the Closet in 1735 on the death of the man whose deputy he had been, and died on 1 April 1746. He was the father of John, Bishop of Durham 1771–87 (who married a daughter of the Duke of Kent), and was the grandfather of the last two earls of Bridgwater.

JOSEPH BUTLER (1692–1752) was the youngest of the eight children of a well-to-do draper of Wantage (Berkshire), who had prospered in his business and retired while still quite young to a large house called the Priory on the edge of the town. Mr Butler intended his son for the Presbyterian ministry, and after a short time at the local grammar school sent him to a dissenting academy at Gloucester, which later removed to Tewkesbury. Among his fellow pupils there was Thomas Secker, the future Archbishop of Canterbury, with whom Butler formed a lifelong friendship. Sixteen pupils studied at the academy at the time, with logic,

Hebrew, mathematics and the classics in the curriculum; that he was mastering his subjects is clear from some correspondence he carried on, while still at Tewkesbury, with Samuel Clarke the philosopher, who apparently specialised in discussions with able young men. Butler was twenty-one when he wrote to Clarke in November 1713 challenging two arguments by which the latter, in lectures a few years before, had set out to demonstrate the existence and attributes of God. The young man's obvious candour and ability clearly made an impression on Clarke.

By now Butler had decided to conform to the Church of England and persuaded his father to allow him to enter Oriel College, Oxford, in March 1714, but it seems that he was never wholly satisfied with the university of his choice, referring scornfully to 'frivolous lectures' and 'unintelligible disputations' by which he was 'quite tired out'. A threat to migrate to Cambridge was not carried out because a growing friendship with Edward Talbot, son of the Bishop of Salisbury, led to his ordination in 1718. A few months later he received the appointment as Preacher at the Rolls Chapel in London, a post, as Gilbert Burnet found, which led to higher things.

Sadly, Edward Talbot died only eighteen months later, but on his deathbed he commended his friend to his father. The bishop, who moved from Salisbury to Durham in 1721, amply responded to the commendation. Butler received a prebend at Salisbury, followed by a living near Darlington and in 1725 the 'golden' rectory of Stanhope in Weardale. Thus, at the age of thirty-three Butler was at last of independent means.

At Stanhope he developed a secluded lifestyle. He was remembered there for the black pony he rode either 'very fast' or, 'falling into reveries', allowing it to graze at will. He was at the time immensely preoccupied with the writing of his famous *Analogy of Religion*, which was published in 1736. He dedicated the work to his late friend Edward Talbot's brother Charles, Lord Talbot of Hensol, the Lord Chancellor, saying that it was in recognition of 'the highest obligations to Lord Talbot's father', the late Bishop of Durham. The Chancellor, who had made Butler his chaplain on assuming office in 1733, promptly gave him a prebendal stall at Rochester, which he was permitted to hold with his Salisbury one.

Butler had thus, through the Talbot connection, begun to be well known; one who was 'always so courteous and kind', as Edward Talbot had described him, as well as being a fine preacher and a learned divine. Queen Caroline, whose influence in ecclesiastical affairs was considerable, became interested in him and would 'command his attendance every evening from 7 till 9'. She made him her Clerk of the Closet, an indication of the personal character of the title, and he remained close to her until her death on 20 November 1737.

Earlier in that year the Queen had commended Butler personally to Archbishop Potter, then newly-enthroned at Canterbury, and soon after her death Butler preached before the King on 'profiting from affliction', his hearer, perhaps remarkably, being much affected and promising to 'do something good for him'. The good turned out to be the offer of the bishopric of Bristol, which was not at all to Butler's liking. He accepted grudgingly, but typically commented in a letter to Walpole (28 August 1738) that 'it was not very suitable either to the conditions of my fortune nor to the recommendation with which I was honoured'. The bishopric was, in fact, the poorest in England, but Butler was allowed to retain his prebend at Rochester and his rectory at Stanhope so as to supplement his income (*in commendam* was the phrase used, rather than 'in plurality'). Within two years he was given the deanery of St Paul's, another Crown appointment, but then he had to give up both the rectory and the prebend.

The well-known interview with John Wesley was early in his time at Bristol and was also at the beginning of Wesley's career as an itinerant preacher. Wesley's sermons were already leading to some of the phenomena which the rational person that was Butler would inevitably find distasteful. Hence the famous remark: 'Sir, the pretending to special revelations of the Holy Spirit is a horrid thing, a very horrid thing.' Furthermore he recommended Wesley, Anglican priest though he was, to leave his diocese; advice which the young preacher did not take. In fact, of course, Bristol became one of the great centres of Methodism, with Wesley's Chapel, the New Room in the Horsefair, eventually becoming a mecca for Methodists the world over.

Butler himself remained in Bristol for twelve years, spending much time and money in improving the Palace. Some reports have it that he devoted the whole income of the see to the task every year of the twelve he was there. He certainly did much work on the chapel, among other things placing a slab of black marble with an inlaid cross in white marble over the existing altar. His work survived until destruction during the Bristol riots of 1831.

In 1746 he succeeded Egerton as Clerk of the Closet, and when Archbishop Potter died in 1747 an offer of the primacy was made to him. He declined it, believing it was 'too late for him to try and support a falling church', but he accepted the Crown's invitation in 1750 to the see of Durham. He was only to enjoy his new appointment for two years, and died on 16 June 1752. He was remembered in the north for his great liberality, entertaining the principal gentry three times a week, and subscribing almost recklessly to charities. One tale survives of his receiving a request for some good cause and immediately finding out from his steward how much money he had in the house. 'Five hundred pounds, my Lord,' replied the steward. 'Give it to them,' said the bishop, 'it's a shame that I have so much.' When he died he gave £200 to his chaplain and large sums to missionary and medical work, the remainder going to his nephews and nieces – the total sum left amounting to about £10,000. He directed that all his papers and sermons be burnt 'without being read by anyone', and that request seems to have been carried out. He did, however, leave a lasting name as one of the greatest exponents of natural theology and ethics in England since the Reformation.

NOTES

Biographies based on entries in *Dictionary of National Biography*, supplemented by *Complete Peerage*, ii. 311–16 for Bishop Egerton and the memorial inscription in Salisbury Cathedral to Bishop Burnet. See also N.W. Wraxall, *Historical Memoirs of his Own Time* (4 vols. 1836).

1. *Portland MSS.*, (Historical MSS. Commission), vii. 260–1.
2. *The Present State of the British Court* (1720), 48–9.
3. British Library, Egerton MS. 1708, f. 400.
4. *Portland MSS.*, vii. 380.
5. Ibid., 461.
6. British Library, Additional MSS. 36056, f. 137; 36057, f. 97b.

CHAPTER SIX

UNPROFITABLE AND UNWORTHY SERVANTS

T HE CLERKS IN the eighty years after the death of Bishop Butler were, perhaps inevitably, lesser men whose personal attractions have sometimes been difficult to recognise. Both Thomas and Hurd were preachers and courtiers; both acted as tutors to successive Princes of Wales, and might reasonably have expected to retain those close links with the Royal Family when their erstwhile pupils wore the crown. Politics and social connections brought Gilbert and Pelham to royal notice, though any more pleasing qualities have successfully evaded the searches of their biographers. Carr, as vicar of Brighton, found himself the acceptable parish priest of the Prince Regent, and his care was duly rewarded so long as his sovereign lived. The fall of the Tory government in 1830 as well as the death of George IV brought him and his fellow Tory bishops under pressure, a pressure which ended in his removal from office on the accession of Queen Victoria, the first Clerk removed for obvious political reasons since the departure of Thomas Sprat in 1688.

JOHN GILBERT (1693–1761) owed more to family and social connections than to his own abilities. Son of a prebendary of Exeter, he went to Trinity College, Oxford, and then transferred to Merton. He reached the primacy of York in 1757 having held successively (and sometimes concurrently) the vicarage of Ashburton (Devon), an Exeter Chapter living, his late father's prebendal stall at Exeter, followed by the sub-deanery and then the deanery there. He was in addition a canon of Christ Church, Oxford, from 1740 Bishop of Llandaff, and from 1748 Bishop of Salisbury. By the time he became Archbishop his health was failing and he languished, rather than lived, 'through a pontificate of four years, when he sank under a complication of infirmities'. He died in 1761.

Gilbert was appointed to succeed the great Bishop Butler as Clerk in 1752 while he was still at Salisbury, and remained in office until his translation to York. He also held the offices of Almoner and Chancellor of the Order of the Garter. Yet he seems to have possessed few qualifications to justify his high promotion in the Church, being neither a scholar nor a theologian. Graces of character might have made up for these deficiencies, but apparently he was not blessed with them either. He engaged in an unseemly brawl with the civic mace-bearer in Salisbury during the course of his enthronement procession, seeking to wrench the mace from his hands on the grounds that within the Cathedral Close the Mayor had no jurisdiction, an incident that can hardly have endeared him to the city. Indeed, Horace Walpole, never very fond of the clergy, described him as 'composed of that common mixture of ignorance, meanness and arrogance'.

Interestingly, Gilbert's method of administering the rite of Confirmation has been re-introduced to some extent in our own day, for he was the first bishop to make a practice of laying his hands on each candidate as he moved along the altar rails, and then retiring to the altar to pronounce the prayer solemnly for the whole number.

Yet another graduate of Christ Church, Oxford, JOHN THOMAS (1696–1781) succeeded John Gilbert as Clerk when the latter was translated to York in 1757. The new Clerk's father, a Colonel in the Brigade of Guards, sent his son to the Charterhouse, and at the age of twenty-four he became a fellow of All Souls and took a curacy in London 'having been disappointed of a living promised to him by a friend of his father'.

Good, however, came of the London appointment, for his preaching began to draw crowds and he was soon given a prebendal stall in St Paul's Cathedral and the living of St Benet and St Peter, Paul's Wharf, which he held for twenty-four years.

Thomas was made a royal chaplain by King George II in 1742, having attracted the King's attention while he was still Prince of Wales. Five years later he was made Bishop of Peterborough, and he stayed there (still keeping his London parish) for ten years, but he combined the duties of the see from 1752 with those of tutor to the Prince of Wales. He seems, nevertheless, to have been a conscientious bishop, although Hurd, his successor as Clerk, damned him with faint praise by calling him 'Honest John'. He is credited with some scholarship and 'a taste in letter writing'. In 1757 he was translated to Salisbury, and in 1761 to Winchester. There he remained for the next twenty years; at his death at the age of eighty-five he had been on the episcopal bench for thirty-four years and Clerk for twenty-four.

RICHARD HURD had just a month more to serve as Bishop of Lichfield and Coventry when he was sworn Clerk in May 1781. He was the son of a substantial Staffordshire farmer and became, as well as a bishop, a writer and literary critic of great distinction. Indeed, the fact that he was, for over thirty years, bishop of two sees and was even offered the primacy seems, in the opinion of those who assessed his life and work soon after his death, to have been of secondary importance to his skills as an author. Gibbon himself knew 'few writers more deserving of the great, though prostituted name of the critic'. Excessive as this praise may be, Hurd ought to be remembered for his *Letters on Chivalry and Romance* (1762), which helped to initiate the Romantic Movement in their discussion of knight-errantry and Gothic literature and art.

His sermons, his lectures, and his courtly manner caught the attention of those in high places. Appointed Preacher at Lincoln's Inn in 1765 and two years later Archdeacon of Gloucester, he delivered the first Warburton Lectures in 1772 under the title 'An Introduction to the Study of the Prophecies concerning the Christian Church, and in particular concerning the Church of Papal Rome'. Within four years they had gone into four editions, and they were reprinted as long afterwards as 1839 by the Revd Edward Bickersteth, a leading Evangelical divine who was much concerned over Papal claims at the time of the Catholic Revival in the Church of England.

At the end of 1774 Hurd was nominated to the see of Lichfield, and on 5 June 1776 was appointed Preceptor to the Prince of Wales and the Duke of York. The latter still called him Bishop of Lichfield nearly twenty-five years later, although Hurd was translated to Worcester on John Thomas's death in 1781. More than once in the surviving correspondence between the King and Hurd, the Bishop asked after the Duke's health, and other letters reveal the growing intimacy between the Clerk and the Royal Family. Often he wrote to thank the King for presents of books, usually the Latin prize essays from Gottingen (one in 1785 was on suicide, but still in good Latin), although more than once he apologised for not having time to read them. At Christmas 1784 he was expected at Windsor, but four years later the role was reversed. The King and Queen decided to visit the Clerk: 'the joy it will give me to welcome my royal visitors to this old-fashioned place [Hartlebury Castle], but therefore the better suited to an old Bishop [he was sixty-eight] if Your Majesty will not like it the less for being plain and unadorned.'

Hurd's age and his inability through declining health to do the duties of his office as Clerk clearly distressed him. 'Nothing is so painful to me,' he wrote in 1792, 'in this decline of life as my total inability to perform my several duties . . . and in particular to wait in person on his Majesty on every occasion that calls upon me to give that attendance.' He marvelled in

1797 at the King's 'goodness to an old unprofitable servant', and in 1800 was delighted to receive from the King a New Year greeting and later a letter in the King's own hand, which 'raised the greatest emotion'. The appointment from 1800 of one and later four Deputy Clerks alleviated his distress, and he continued to take an interest in affairs, commenting in 1801 on what a 'fine action' it had been to have a Thanksgiving for the King's recovery, although he regretted that he 'could not be a witness, at least, of this hallowed scene, and that the unworthy Clerk of your Majesty's Closet is wholly disabled from bearing a part in it'.

'My bodily weakness is not the worst,' he wrote later in 1801. 'My memory is almost entirely gone, and my powers of attention so weak that conversation . . . is almost too much for me . . . I . . . employ the little recollection I am master of in calling to mind the innumerable obligations I have to your Majesty . . . ' Yet Hurd lived on, never considering resignation, and he was doubtless most excited when the King suggested that, in face of possible invasion in 1803, the Royal Family should be removed to Worcester. In 1804 Hurd approved the names of two more Deputy Clerks and wished the King 'Happy Returns' for his birthday. Another Royal visit to Worcester was projected in 1805 and Hurd expressed the wish to see his 'most beloved and indulgent Sovereign' again. In the event the King did not go, and the poor old man must have been disappointed. Perhaps it was some compensation that the Archbishop of Canterbury, Charles Manners Sutton, should have driven over from Cheltenham to see the oldest bishop on the bench. Hurd himself had refused the primacy when Frederick Cornwallis died in 1783, and now he met Cornwallis's successor-but-one, a man who himself had been a bishop since 1792 and whom Hurd had never met!

Horace Walpole described Hurd as 'a gentle, plausible man, affecting a singular decorum which endeared him highly to devout old ladies'. In 1795 Hannah More, equally devout but not yet old, sought a subscription from him for her *Repository Tracts*. These were pious tales designed to offset the revolutionary writings then so prevalent, but Hurd hesitated, warning 'these good ladies and good bishops who would have the poor taught to read, with good design no doubt' that having been taught they could read 'bad books as well as good ones'. Hurd's comments were made, however, in a private letter, not in a public statement; he was intelligent enough to see the inevitability of education permeating through society.

George III's 'dear good Bishop' eventually died at his home at Hartlebury on 28 May 1808 at the age of eighty-eight. In his prolonged absence from Court the Deputy Clerks had evidently worked well in his name; but now the peculiar role of the Clerk became apparent, for the Sovereign's illness prevented him from making such a personal appointment, and the Regent could not make it for him. Thus for five years the Deputies performed the formal duties and the office of Clerk remained vacant. The *Royal Kalendar* for the years 1810 and 1811 record J. Chamberlayne as Clerk of the King's Closet, evidently an error since he was actually Keeper of the King's Drawings and Medals.[1] The office of Clerk was finally filled by April 1813 by the appointment of WILLIAM JACKSON (1751–1815), Bishop of Oxford since the previous year.

He had been a canon of Christ Church, where he and his more famous brother, Cyril, had been undergraduates. William entered the college at seventeen, and became successively tutor, 'rhetoric reader' and censor, before becoming Regius Professor of Greek when he was only thirty-two. (Cyril, who became Dean of Christ Church, was even more wedded to Oxford and academic life, and actually refused both the archbishopric of Armagh and, in 1805, the primatial see of Canterbury). In 1792 William was appointed to the prebend of Dulcote in Wells Cathedral by Bishop Charles Moss, and he held it until his appointment to the see of Oxford in 1812. No record of his activities as Clerk has been found, and the only adjective to describe Jackson which has survived the years is 'self-indulgent'. He died at his Palace at Cuddesdon in the year of Waterloo.

GEORGE PELHAM (1766–1827), Jackson's successor, was the third and youngest son of the first Earl of Chichester. As a young man he went briefly into the Guards, but soon forsook the army for the Church, and went to Clare College, Cambridge. As scion of a leading Whig family he was quickly promoted, getting a prebendal stall and a residentiary canonry at Chichester shortly after his ordination as deacon. He held both preferments until he died. He later added two parochial livings and a stall at Winchester to his tally, provoking the comment to William Cowper, the poet, by a friend that 'young Pelham, at just turned 25, is already in possession of two livings', a remark indicating that even for those days his acquisitions were excessive.

The sorry tale continued: Bishop of Bristol at thirty-seven, he was angling only two years later for the vacant, and more profitable, see of Norwich. His letter to the Prime Minister on 8 February 1805, written from his house in fashionable Welbeck Street, declared that he had heard from so many quarters of his nomination to the vacant bishopric that he could no longer refrain from expressing his gratitude, as it would be a lasting obligation. Lord Liverpool replied by return to the effect that the report had 'arisen without his knowledge and that he could not have the satisfaction of promoting his wishes'.

But Pelham was soon on the move, not to Norwich but to Exeter, by the autumn of 1807, where he held the archdeaconry, the treasurership and a residential stall to add to the perfectly adequate income he had already amassed from Bristol and Chichester. Still he wanted more, but had to wait thirteen years for the senior see of Lincoln, where he remained until he died.

Pelham was made Clerk of the Closet in 1815, during his Exeter years, probably because of his aristocratic connections and his politics. By 1818 it was reported that the Bishop and his wife were in daily attendance at the dinners given by the Prince Regent at the Pavilion in Brighton. His other activities at Court have not been traced, except his attendance at the funeral of the Duke of York in St George's Chapel, Windsor, on a bitter winter's day, 19 January 1827. The cold he caught there turned to pleurisy which proved fatal a fortnight later.

Of this unattractive man it was said in his favour that he was 'punctual in the discharge of business and impartial in his distribution of patronage', an interesting comment when he had spent a lifetime trying to persuade influential people, chiefly the Crown, to be very partial in theirs. Of his wife Mary, whom he had married in 1792, it was remarked that she was haughty in her style, and in the Palace at Exeter 'never rises from her seat to receive her visitors'. He is said to have begged George III to dispense him, on reaching the episcopal bench in 1803, from wearing the traditional wig, but the sovereign refused.

The sycophantic Pelham died at a time of growing political unrest, and it fell to his successor as Clerk, ROBERT JAMES CARR (1774–1841), to be well and truly caught up in it. Carr was the son of a Twickenham schoolmaster who himself gave his son his primary education and later secured for him a place at Worcester College, Oxford. After ordination in 1798 he held some important livings before becoming vicar of Brighton. There he attracted the attention of the Prince Regent, whose Pavilion was then at the height of its glittering social fame. The young vicar became a close friend of the future King, who on his accession to the throne in 1820 made Carr Dean of Hereford, in 1821 Deputy Clerk of the Closet, and three years later Bishop of Chichester. He was, therefore, the obvious choice as Clerk of the Closet on Pelham's death. But in only three years, on 26 June 1830, he was attending at his sovereign's deathbed.

In November 1830, with the new King William IV barely crowned, and news of the 1830 revolution in France stirring public opinion, the almost permanent Tory government fell, and a Whig cabinet under Earl Grey came into office. The Duke of Wellington, in his last act as Prime Minister, hastily filled some ecclesiastical vacancies, elevating Dr Henry Philpotts to Exeter where he carried extreme Tory principles into every aspect of Church affairs for thirty years. Carr was moved to Worcester in fulfilment of a promise made by the late King on his deathbed.

There were now danger signals ahead for the Church. The Reform Bill brought in by the new government passed the House of Commons in September 1831, but Grey was not confident it would pass the Lords. He therefore tried to influence the Bishops, most of whom had been appointed under Tory governments. It was to no avail; when the Lords' vote came on

8 October only Maltby, the new Bishop of Chichester hurriedly appointed by Grey, and the aged Bathurst of Norwich (by proxy, and he had anyway probably not grasped what the Bill was about) voted with the government. The Archbishop of Canterbury and twenty of his fellow bishops went into the Noes lobby. The bishops' votes constituted half the total by which the Bill was lost.

Carr was actually among the six bishops who abstained, he for the reason that though a Tory himself he owed his elevation to the new Whig Prime Minister. But abstainer though he was, he did not escape the tide of popular rage against the House of Lords, and most particularly against the bishops. Whig and Radical newspapers pilloried them as maintainers of graft and bribery, enemies of liberty and the civil rights of Englishmen, and their wealth and state were denounced (they were 'paid £528,698 per annum for keeping liberty from the people'). They were charged with voting against reform, or in Carr's case not having the courage to vote for it, because they owed their income to corruption and must therefore defend corruption; with revelling in fashionable luxury at their palaces while they knew nothing of the labourer's cottage.

Within days of the defeat of the Bill it was a harassing matter to be a bishop. On 11 October a mob of 8,000 in Carlisle burnt theirs in effigy in the market place; the Bishop of Llandaff kept 'a brown greatcoat and round hat' in readiness for a possible escape from the back of his house across the fields. On 24 October, while the Bishop of Bath and Wells was consecrating a church in Bedminster, a suburb of Bristol, a crowd waited outside to waylay him and stoned his carriage as he drove away. He pulled up the drawbridge at his Palace in Wells that night.

Lord Grey lost no time in seeking to win over the bishops to the cause of reform, judging that it could not be in their interests or for the good of the Church that they should be castigated in public. Calling on Bishop Blomfield of London in November 1831 he extracted from him an admission that he regretted the course which the bishops had taken and persuaded him to undertake to vote for the new Bill. Grey was less successful with the weak and vacillating Archbishop Howley, but tried to persuade the King to influence the bishops, perhaps using Bishop Carr because of his link with the Crown for so long.

The Prime Minister's lobbying was successful. When the second reading of the new Bill was finally carried on 13 April 1832 twelve bishops voted in favour, and the Clerk of the Closet was among them. Reform in the Church was now as much on everybody's lips as reform of the law affecting the liberty of the citizen, and *The Times* leader of 2 October 1832 declared: 'The establishment of the Church is now in peril, and that peril becomes every hour more imminent'. In the same month Dr Thomas Arnold of Rugby could declare: 'The Church as it now stands no human power can save.'

But the Clerk of the Closet kept his royal appointment through it all. His political activities seem to have been more significant than personal anecdote, but he is remembered for his part in freeing bishops from the discomfort of their wigs. 'Would it be possible,' Bishop Blomfield wrote, 'to ask the King if we could dispense with our wigs?' The Clerk, like Pelham before him, made the attempt, but George IV would have none of it. Blomfield tried again directly, with William IV, one hot summer day at Brighton. 'In this tropical season I find my episcopal wig an encumbrance,' he told the King. Back came the royal reply: 'Tell the Bishop he is not to wear a wig on my account; I dislike it as much as he does, and shall be glad to see the whole bench wear their own hair.' That signalled the death-knell of bewigged bishops, the last to wear one in Church being Archbishop Sumner right up to his death in 1862. Bishop Carr actually clung to his wig, but lost his office as Clerk of the Closet on the accession of Queen Victoria in 1837, dismissed 'on account of a strict adherence to his political principles'. He remained Bishop of Worcester until his death at Hartlebury Castle in 1841.

NOTES

Biographies based on entries in *Dictionary of National Biography*. Supplementary material on Bishop Hurd from: *Correspondence of King George III (1760–83)*, ed. the Hon. Sir John Fortescue (1928); *The Later Correspondence of George III*, ed. A. Aspinall (1962).

CHAPTER SEVEN

THE QUEEN'S BISHOPS

T HE FOUR MEN who served as Clerks of the Closet under Queen
Victoria stand out as a new generation of men far removed from the
High Tory mould of so many of their predecessors. Better known
as individuals than many Clerks before them, they were chosen by the
Queen herself (and, while he lived, also by Prince Albert) for their personal
qualities, and for the special gifts that each could bring to the office bearing
in mind their churchmanship and political views. Furthermore, Randall
Davidson, the last of the four, was the man who in his own person
transformed the holder of the office into the Queen's most influential
adviser on Church affairs, and by retaining that same influence when he
became Archbishop of Canterbury, had the effect of diminishing very
considerably the position and power which the Clerk had over the
centuries so often held at Court.

Early in 1837 Lord Melbourne nominated the admirable Whig pastor of
Alderley in Cheshire, EDWARD STANLEY (1779–1849), to the see of
Norwich, vacant at last by the death of Henry Bathurst in his ninety-fourth
year. King William IV told the Prime Minister that he much approved of
the choice, saying what great value he attached to the exemplary discharge
of the duties of a parish priest, and adding that he rejoiced when a man like
Stanley combined with this virtue that of a good family, gentlemanly
habits and literary and scientific pursuits.

Stanley did, indeed, belong to a new generation of bishops who readily
absorbed the political ethos which was fast ousting Tory paternalism as the
most prominent feature of episcopal thought. The new bishop turned out
to be more outspoken than anyone had expected. He began by inviting
Dr Arnold to preach the sermon at his consecration in Lambeth Palace
chapel. Archbishop Howley promptly refused, saying that although he

respected the great man he could not allow him to preach because it would be so ill-received by the clergy. In reply to the Archbishop, Stanley refused to choose anyone else, so a chaplain was appointed to preach. At the installation shortly afterwards in Norwich Cathedral, Stanley had 1,200 charity children placed on scaffolding before the altar, each school with a different flag. The mayor and corporation did not approve, nor did many of the clergy present that day to greet their new bishop.

Stanley had a consuming passion, like Arnold, for Christian education: 'Christian education alone,' he wrote in a Charge delivered to his clergy in 1838, 'deserves the name of education; it is through Christian education only that we can hope to see the social and political condition of our countrymen purified and perfected.' In another context he could advocate 'education even when not Christian education' for 'conscientious dissent is neither sinful nor schismatic'. Those were strong views, arousing strong opposition, and Melbourne received little credit among the clergy for nominating such a liberal, almost heretical, bishop. Yet in a sermon preached in St Paul's Cathedral on 19 May 1843 before the Society for the Propagation of the Gospel in Foreign Parts, a copy of which he sent to Buckingham Palace in July,[1] he argued powerfully for the Established Church as being 'preferable to any other religious system left to the change and caprice of times and circumstances'. He went on to declare that 'what is chiefly wanted in the present day is a steady, constant spirit of well-regulated and well-balanced charity, not dependent on temporary excitements', since 'the duty of carrying out the Gospel to heathen lands is no casual emergency, but a perpetual unchanging demand'.

Stanley had a courageous and engaging manner. The young Queen Victoria was captivated by him, sending for him first to Windsor after she had read his installation sermon, and then to the flamboyant (and for her alien) surroundings of the Royal Pavilion at Brighton. She had come to the view that what the bishop was saying and meaning 'pointed in the direction all good Christians ought to go'.[2] It was, indeed, Stanley's broad approach to matters of belief and practice that the Queen liked. A letter to him from George Anson, the Queen's Private Secretary, dated 24 July 1843, about the formation of the National Society (for Education) 'to supply the wants of the poor in the manufacturing towns' reported that the Queen had given £1,000 and the Prince £500 upon the assurance given by the Archbishop that those sums should not fall exclusively into the hands of the Puseyite party. 'Your name,' Anson went on, 'will carry great weight with those who form a dislike to extreme views . . . and might (otherwise) refuse to join this nationally important undertaking.' Stanley had to be seen to be involved 'as a guarantee that a proper balance would be maintained'.[3]

The breadth of Stanley's interests also fascinated the Queen: gymnastics, botany, mineralogy, entomology – all were grist to his mill; and his ornithological observations were published under the title *Familiar History of Birds, their Nature, Habits and Instincts* (2 Volumes, 1836). He was one of the first clergymen to lecture on the then suspect science of geology. This broad-minded man suited the Queen better than any traditional Tory.

Once he became a bishop, after no less than thirty-two years in the family living of Alderley, Stanley turned his innovative mind to Church reform. Non-residence, pluralities and scarcity of services were among the many abuses he tackled in his large diocese. Examinations for ordination began to be carefully conducted, and the bishop made it his business to become personally acquainted with the previous career of every candidate for Holy Orders. He appointed seventy Rural Deans to keep him in touch with what was going on all over his diocese; and he entertained them all every year in the Palace at Norwich. At great personal expense he prosecuted and removed those clergyman who had fallen foul of the law. Instead of confirming once in seven years at a few large centres, he began annual confirmations in convenient churches. He became involved in Bible societies, city missions, poor law administration, ragged schools. Always an eager advocate of temperance, he appeared on platforms up and down his diocese to support all who stood against the drunkenness of the times. There seemed no end to his enthusiasm and capacity for hard work, characteristics which initially earned the suspicion of the leading clergy and laymen. By the end of his twelve years in office, both as bishop and Clerk of the Closet, he had won the greatest affection of all classes of society and had changed for the good the whole atmosphere of religious life throughout East Anglia. He died on 6 September 1849.

Queen Victoria's second Clerk was JOHN GRAHAM (1794–1865), a member of Christ's College, Cambridge, who did extremely well in both Classics and Mathematics, becoming Fourth Wrangler and sharing the Chancellor's Medal. Fellow and Tutor from 1816 and from 1830 Master of his old college, he was elected Vice-Chancellor in the following year. On 26 January 1841 he was nominated chaplain to Prince Albert, with whom he must have shared interests in mathematics and science, and he took a prominent and delicate part in the successful campaign of 1847 to have the Prince elected Chancellor of Cambridge University. Was it this support which resulted in Graham's appointment as Bishop of Chester in 1848, and in the year after that as Clerk of the Closet to the sovereign?

Graham was obviously much loved in Cambridge, seat of his academic labours for more than thirty years. When he left the city for Chester, the mayor and corporation gave him an address of congratulation on his appointment, the only recorded instance of such an honour having been bestowed by town upon gown.

Graham's politics were liberal. Prince Albert liked bishops that way, though the Queen also had a penchant for Evangelicals. He spoke and voted very rarely in the House of Lords and opted for a very simple lifestyle. His main aim was peace – peace in his diocese, peace among men generally. In consequence his approach to the dissenters of Chester was always conciliatory, an attitude which resulted in some opposition from his high church clergy. The Queen respected him greatly, no doubt much influenced by the friendship between him and Prince Albert. After the Prince's death Graham was thus a link with those golden years when the Sovereign and her husband were together. Bishop Graham died on 15 June 1865.

Graham's successor was also made Clerk because of Prince Albert. Indeed, HENRY PHILPOTT (1807–1892), Master of St Catharine's College, Cambridge, was Vice-Chancellor of the university in 1847 and in that capacity received the Queen and the Prince Consort when the latter was installed as Chancellor. From then on Philpott was in close touch with the Court, serving as chaplain to the Chancellor and acting as his 'University Correspondent'. In that last capacity he kept the Prince informed about university gossip, as a result of which the new Chancellor in his characteristic way gradually made his own suggestions, winning over the many in the university who had resented 'the student of Saxe-Gotha' being put at their head. In 1861 Philpott was nominated to the see of Worcester, and on John Graham's death in 1865 he succeeded him as Clerk.

Three times elected Vice-Chancellor of Cambridge and therefore a very considerable figure in both city and university life, his subsequent career as a diocesan bishop was uneventful. He thoroughly disliked public life, seldom attended the House of Lords, never took part in the deliberations of the Upper House of Convocation, and is said to have made only a single appearance at the private meetings of the bishops. He did not allow diocesan conferences because he 'had a horror of irresponsible talk'.

As the years passed Philpott gained the reputation of being much the most old-fashioned bishop on the bench. He had so little to do with his cathedral chapter that as late as 1886 one of the residentiary canons was quite astonished at being asked to be an examining chaplain to his bishop. He was, however, rather ahead of his time in refusing to support the dean and chapter when they objected in 1875 to the Three Choirs Festival continuing to take over the cathedral every three years. The chapter said that the music should be part of a service and that admission should be free to the poor. That year's festival was held only with organ and choir, and at the next one, in 1878, the chosen oratorio had to be in a service, and the scaffolding for the choirs was not erected.

At eighty-three and with a sick wife Philpott resigned from his see, but Queen Victoria accepted his sad request – sad because he was not physically up to it – that he continue as Clerk, surely a mark of the affection that existed between them. The Queen's Private Secretary made the suggestion to the Queen that Randall Davidson be appointed Assistant Clerk to carry out the duties.[4] Philpott agreed and retired to his beloved Cambridge, where he died on 10 January 1892, having been for thirty years Bishop of Worcester and for twenty-six Clerk of the Closet.

The Queen had for long been quite clear who should succeed the aged Bishop of Worcester, and with the appointment to the Clerkship of her already beloved counsellor, RANDALL THOMAS DAVIDSON, Bishop of Rochester, the office was to change dramatically. She continued to rely on him as she had done ever since she had made him Dean of Windsor nearly ten years earlier, and she was to retain her enormous regard for his judgement until the day of her death. By then he was within a year of becoming Archbishop of Canterbury, and when King Edward VII at long last came to the throne, Davidson simply continued the role which the now middle-aged king had long been accustomed to his filling with such distinction. So the adviser to the King on spiritual matters was from then on perfectly naturally the Archbishop of Canterbury, and not the Clerk of the Closet.

Randall Davidson was born to Scottish parents in 1848 and baptised in the Church of Scotland, but he came to Harrow for his education and was confirmed there as an Anglican. Partly through being accidentally shot in the back when he was still at school, he did badly at Oxford, but he then set about learning some theology as he had made up his mind to be ordained. He served as an earnest curate for three years at Dartford (Kent) whence he was rescued to be the resident chaplain to the Archbishop of Canterbury. The link was his Oxford friendship with Archbishop Tait's only (and later invalid) son, Crawfurd.

'I am now bound to see and do everything,' Davidson wrote to his father after a few weeks. 'I am certainly enjoying my life here hugely and making many friends.' One of them soon became his lifelong companion, for early in 1878 he proposed to his master's daughter Edith, who from then on was to be a wonderful wife and hostess in the succession of large houses her husband took them to upon his ecclesiastical way.

Very soon the ageing Archbishop was using his chaplain to write letters and conduct negotiations beyond Davidson's wildest dreams of a few years before. Honoured by a chaplaincy to the Queen when he was only thirty-one, he was nominated as her Sub-Almoner before the Archbishop died, and when on the strength of that royal appointment he ventured to write to Her Majesty to describe Tait's death he had a swift reply ('might [I] have a little of his hair?') and an invitation to go and see her: 'Would it suit you to come and see me on Saturday, either at ¼ to 3 or ½ past 5? I am most anxious to make your acquaintance having heard so much about you.'

The interview on 9 December 1882 was to have far-reaching effects. The Queen wrote in her Journal: 'Saw Mr Davidson, the Arch Bishop's son-in-law, and was seldom more struck than I have been by his personality . . . We went over various topics, and I feel that Mr Davidson is a man who may be of great use to me, for which I am truly thankful.' 'What on earth has been happening?' asked Sir Henry Ponsonby, the Queen's Private Secretary, when Davidson eventually emerged. 'I don't know when the Queen has had such a long interview with anybody.' 'She certainly startled me,' said the awestruck young priest, 'by the openness of her confidence and her genuine anxiety to hear all that I had to say.' The Private Secretary wrote next day to Gladstone, the Prime Minister: 'The Queen was very much struck with Mr Davidson with whom she had a long interview yesterday. He is singularly pleasing both in appearance and manner, very sympathetic, and evidently very intelligent, wise and able.'

Very soon Davidson was advising the Queen against appointing the Bishop of Winchester (Browne) to succeed Tait at Canterbury; and recommending various names instead. His twenty years of influential counselling had begun, as the Queen herself acknowledged in a letter to him just before Christmas: 'As there will be two vacancies on the Episcopal Bench and a Deanery (if not two!) I should be *most thankful* if you could *help* me with names . . . but losing, as I have done, the two dear Deans, Stanley [of Westminster] and Wellesley [of Windsor], I am left without any one to turn to for advice and help . . . and I feel you have had such immense opportunities of knowing *all* the Clergy that I could *not* look to *any* one *more likely* to help me than yourself.'

It was not long before the Queen's Private Secretary was permitted to establish a short cypher code with him for use in cases of necessity! In May 1883 the Queen wrote to Archbishop Benson, himself only a few months in office, about her choice of the man to be made Dean of Windsor: 'I myself, can think of no one more fitted than Mr Davidson (if you could give him up!) from his great knowledge of *society* and of the Clergy generally, and his great charm of manner. The only thing that might be said against his appointment is his youth. But surely that is a fault which recedes quickly, and he has had so much experience, and is so much liked – that I should think this would be no insurmountable obstacle.' Interestingly, the Archbishop replied: 'With regard to his youth – I think Your Majesty can wholly set aside whatever might be said about that. His youth has all the advantage of spring and freshness, while it does not carry him away into any intemperate expression even, at any time – much less into rashness.' Davidson was appointed – at thirty-five years old (and with a twenty-four year old wife) the youngest Dean anyone could remember.

The Queen's high regard for him was soon to be severely tested. John Brown, the Highland servant who in some ways had been a substitute for Prince Albert, died; and within a few months she was proposing to publish a further volume of her Journal, which contained many highly personal references to the faithful Brown. Davidson, knowing that the first volume of the Journal had caused many raised eyebrows, was fearful of the effect of a second, a view shared by many others in the Court circle. Those others were afraid to express as much, and it fell to the Dean to be as tactful and firm in the matter as he could: '. . . Your Majesty will readily understand that such a spirit of ready response to the gracious confidences so frankly given, is not always to be found, and I should be deceiving Your Majesty were I not to admit that there are, especially among the humbler classes, some, (perhaps it would be true to say *many*) who do not show themselves worthy of those confidences, and whose spirit, judging by their published periodicals, is one of such unappreciative criticism as I should not desire Your Majesty to see.'

That was a very brave letter indeed for a young subject and direct employee to write to his Sovereign, and Davidson did not have long to wait for the Queen's reaction. She asked for a withdrawal and an apology, but the Dean offered his resignation instead. This time absolutely nothing happened, but a fortnight later the Queen asked to see the Dean on quite another matter, and the proposed book was not mentioned then or subsequently. The implication was clear: the Sovereign had seen the wisdom of her subject. It is safe to say that for the rest of her life the Queen's belief in Randall Davidson as a man, her dependence on his counsel in the affairs of the Church, and her confidence in his general ministry and judgement were unwavering.

Before long Archbishop Benson was saying in private letters to the Queen, and the Queen in return, that the Dean should soon be a bishop. They recognised his ambition, but were sure that their opinions of his star qualities were right. Lord Salisbury gave him the choice of either Worcester or Rochester, both more modest sees than Winchester which was also under discussion and which the Queen would have preferred him to be offered. The Prime Minister assumed he would choose Worcester 'as being connected with a more stirring and influential population' (the diocese then included Birmingham), but he chose Rochester on the grounds that he already knew its clergy from his days at Lambeth. The Queen herself began to have second thoughts. Writing as she sometimes did in the third person, she confessed to Davidson 'that She has (excepting in one case, the Bishop of Ripon) never found people promoted to the Episcopate remain what they were before. She hopes and thinks this will not be the case with the Dean. Many who preached so well before, did no longer as Bishops . . . The whole atmosphere of a Cathedral and its surroundings . . . seems to hamper their freedom of speech.' Davidson, indeed, found the wrench difficult; and the Queen's kindness mixed with her obvious regrets made the few months before his consecration very trying. 'The Queen . . . now repents having ever listened to the proposals of raising him to the Bench – for really for his sake as well as for hers she cannot think it is a good thing. . . . She would now wish to mention what she hopes he would be able to do, viz. – always to preach in the Mausoleum once in the summer (this year perhaps the 1st Sunday) – that he would perform the services on the 14th Dec. – and that he would preach once at least in the winter and once in the summer at Osborne. – She hopes he and Mrs Davidson will stay here for 2 nights at the time he does homage.' It was an extraordinary display of affection.

There was one other suggestion for keeping Davidson within the Household. Bishop Philpott's request to retain the Clerkship of the Closet after his resignation of his see in November 1890 had created something of a precedent. It had been understood that Davidson would in some way act as Philpott's deputy in view of the Clerk's poor health, but he felt he could hardly fulfill the duties adequately since he was not then a bishop. By the end of January 1891 it was suggested that he might be a more permanent assistant. Two days later, the Queen's Private Secretary wrote to Philpott enquiring whether, in view of Davidson's impending move from Windsor, 'some Court engagements' might be arranged. In particular, it was suggested that Davidson might deputise for Philpott in a more permanent way than the officially appointed Deputy Clerks.[5]

Davidson was consecrated on St Mark's Day 1891 in Westminster Abbey. Three days later he was gazetted as 'A Clerk of the Closet', a title unique in the history of the office,[6] for Philpott was still Clerk. From then onwards the Queen was constantly requesting his services. If an important post was vacant, she asked Davidson to describe what sort of a man should fill it. When the Prime Minister (whose prerogative it was and still is) suggested a name to her, she telegraphed it in code to her Clerk. Davidson would submit a memorandum, often a long one, in reply. In his old age Davidson was to comment to George Bell, his biographer: 'No senior appointment was made in our Church for the best part of forty years without my approval.' Only Rosebery openly talked of the communications between Davidson and the Queen.

By the time Davidson (from 1895 Bishop of Winchester) became Archbishop of Canterbury the Queen was dead, but King Edward VII renewed his appointment as Clerk on his accession and pointedly expressed the wish to receive just the same counsel from him on all new Church nominations as he had given to the Queen. Within a year, however, Davidson relinquished the Clerkship on becoming Primate of All England; but his influence remained and became a permanent feature of the system.

The Archbishop might no longer be Clerk, but he was invariably consulted. Davidson's closeness to the Sovereign made him arguably the most influential Clerk of the Closet since the seventeenth century when John Earle and Gilbert Burnet had guided the Crown in days of crisis for the Church.

NOTES

The biographies are based on entries in the *Dictionary of National Biography*, with background material from O. Chadwick, *The Victorian Church* (two parts, 1966, 1970). Information on Randall Davidson also from G.K.A. Bell, *Randall Davidson* (3rd edn. 1952)

1. Windsor, Royal Archives, F 37.69.
2. Ibid., Queen Victoria's Journal, 5 October 1837.
3. Ibid., F 37.66.
4. Ibid., Vic. D 13A/148, 153.
5. Ibid., 156.
6. *London Gazette*, 1891, p. 2302.

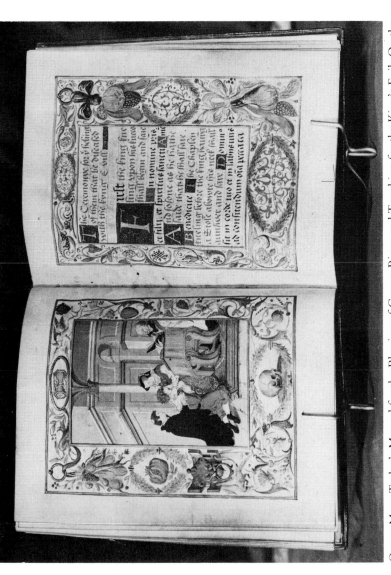

Queen Mary Tudor's Manual for the Blessing of Cramp Rings and Touching for the King's Evil. On the verso of folio 11, shown here on the left, the Queen is depicted at a prayer desk with a sufferer before her and (as the earlier rubric directs) a 'chaplen . . . having a stole abowte his neck'. Behind the patient is the Clerk of the Closet, his tonsured head and black gown suggesting John Ricarde, appointed by the Queen to a stall at Westminster in 1554.

The Manual is owned by Westminster Cathedral, and reproduction is by permission of Monsignor Canon Oliver Kelly, the Administrator. Photograph by Sport and General Press Agency Ltd.

John Dolben (1625–86), Clerk of the Closet to King Charles II 1664–7, Bishop of Rochester 1666, Archbishop of York 1683, with his friends and fellow loyalists (*on left*) John Fell, Dean of Christ Church, and (*on right*) Richard Allestree (1619–81), Canon of Christ Church.

Painting by Sir Peter Lely at Christ Church, Oxford. Reproduced by permission of the Governing Body of Christ Church, Oxford.

Gilbert Burnet (1643–1715), Clerk of the Closet to King William III 1689 and Bishop of Salisbury 1689–1715. The Bishop wears the mantle and holds the purse of office of Chancellor of the Order of the Garter.

Lambeth Palace Collection, probably by Mary Beale. Reproduced by permission of the Archbishop of Canterbury and the Church Commissioners.

Joseph Butler (1692–1752), Clerk of the Closet to King George II 1746–52, Bishop of Bristol 1738–50, Bishop of Durham 1750–52.

Bishop Auckland Castle, English School. Reproduced by permission of the Bishop of Durham and the Church Commissioners.

Randall Thomas Davidson (1848–1930), Clerk of the Closet to Queen Victoria and to King Edward VII 1891–1903, as Dean of Windsor. He was Bishop of Rochester 1891–5 and of Winchester 1895–1903 and Archbishop of Canterbury 1903–28. The Dean wears the Badge of Register of the Order of the Garter.

Painted by Rudolf Svoboda in 1890 at the request of Queen Victoria for the sum of £52 10s. Reproduced by gracious permission of Her Majesty The Queen.

Her Majesty Queen Elizabeth in the grounds of the Bishop's Palace, Norwich, with Percy Mark Herbert (1885–1968), Clerk of the Closet to King George VI and to The Queen 1942–63. He was the first Bishop of Blackburn 1927–42 and Bishop of Norwich 1942–59.

Photograph kindly lent by Mr David Herbert. Eastern Daily Press, Norwich.

The Chapel Royal, St James's Palace, looking south towards the Royal Closet. The Chapel was restored in 1836–7 by Sir Robert Smirke, who entirely refitted the Closet, which was given a new ceiling to match the Tudor work of the rest of the Chapel.

The first ever Badge of Office for the Clerk of the Closet, presented by the Lord Chamberlain at St George's Chapel, Windsor, on the occasion of The Queen's 60th Birthday service, 21 April 1986.

Photograph by I. Kirby, Tisbury.

CHAPTER EIGHT

FRIENDS OF THE FAMILY

T HE INFLUENCE OF Randall Davidson in the councils of Church and State was extraordinary even before he became Primate, and his successors as Clerks, whatever their personal connections with the Royal Family, were never able to emulate the intimacy which had so rapidly grown and splendidly flourished between the young Dean of Windsor and the ageing Queen Victoria. Davidson's successor as Clerk, William Boyd Carpenter, was, in fact, already known to the Queen before Davidson came to Windsor: she once described him as 'a very nice clever little man' and even considered him as a candidate for the deanery.[1] Certainly he became intimate with members of the Royal Family as none of his successors did until Percy Herbert's time; but intimacy did not bring significant influence. Both Boyd Carpenter and Herbert might be described as Court Chaplains, in the mould of John Thomas or Richard Hurd in the eighteenth century who had acted as tutors to successive Princes of Wales; but Hurd once admitted to the King that he had no influence at all with the government and would not comment on appointments to the Bench of Bishops.[2] The other Clerks of the earlier twentieth century were men of stature in different ways, Hubert Burge and Thomas Strong holding the office of Clerk as the culmination of distinguished careers, although Strong's connection with the Royal Family was also close, while Cyril Garbett was to leave the office after six years on his appointment to the Primacy of York and the wider responsibilities of Church leadership. Boyd Carpenter, incidentally, retained the office of Clerk for seven years after his resignation of the see of Ripon, partly because of war conditions and partly because of the Royal Family's natural kindness to long-serving retainers. The Clerkship is held 'during the sovereign's pleasure', and it was very pleasant indeed of the King not to ask this faithful man – or Court toady according to the critics – to surrender the office to a younger and fitter bishop.

67

Like Randall Davidson, WILLIAM BOYD CARPENTER had a long apprenticeship in service to the Crown. He first preached at Windsor before Queen Victoria in June 1877, and the sermon must have made a good impression, for he was invited to preach at St George's each year for the next five years, and then became a canon there. Thus his long association with the Royal Family began. Five thousand letters and forty-two years later he died at Westminster, a fortnight before the First World War ended, still Clerk of the Closet at the age of seventy-seven.

If ever there was a Court Chaplain Boyd Carpenter was that man, but he was many other things besides: social reformer, Biblical preacher, Dante scholar, founder of a liberal theological college, and a diocesan bishop who still found plenty of time to devote to the affairs of the Royal Household. Beginning with that first sermon before the Queen, he preached his eighty-eighth and last twenty-three years later, three weeks before she died; and then there were still eighteen years in which he served her son and grandson. A bond, forged with the sovereign through a common experience of bereavement developed into wide-ranging friendships with the Queen's relations.

In the early days it was Boyd Carpenter, the preacher and consoler, whom the Queen loved. Although bereavement clouded her life permanently after the Prince Consort's death in 1861, her strong sense of duty and her intense interest in public affairs led to the concentration of her sadness at special times and seasons, particularly anniversaries. Very soon after the first interview the Queen granted to him, Boyd Carpenter was permitted to write to her. All his letters were carefully bound, and two volumes were presented to him by King Edward VII after his mother's death. The memory of the dead is the predominating theme: 'I know no one,' the Queen wrote, 'who has more kindly entered into my feelings, and borne with the sinking yearning of my poor wounded heart than you.' So if Davidson became the Queen's adviser on Church appointments and ecclesiastical matters generally, it was Boyd Carpenter who was closest to her spiritually, a Clerk of her Closet without yet the title!

During the course of time the friendship between Bishop (he was given Ripon in 1884) and Sovereign deepened. He entered with heart and soul into the Diamond Jubilee festivities in 1897 and, ardent patriot that he was, he composed special hymns and odes, and wrote articles and eulogies exalting and solemnising various occasions. On the last Sunday of the nineteenth century he was staying at Osborne, and the Queen was not well enough to attend the morning service. But 'she sent me a message asking me to arrange a short service in the afternoon at which she hoped to be present. We had the service in the yellow drawing room, as being more convenient of access than the Chapel. A harmonium was brought in, and H.R.H. Princess Beatrice played . . . I spoke of the changelessness of God from the words: "Thou art the same, and Thy years shall not fail". Then followed Faber's hymn which the Queen liked, "Angels of Jesus, singing to welcome the pilgrims of the night"; and so with as it were the sound of welcoming bells, this last service of the year and the century ended. I saw the Queen once more on the Tuesday. She asked me to come and stay at Cimiez and we fixed the time for my coming. She was not well . . . .' Three weeks later she died.

Boyd Carpenter's standing at Court was very considerable. He had, according to his biographer, 'charming manners, brilliant conversational powers, unfailing solid tact'. Nor was he simply interested in the outward trappings; a striking example of the use he made of his position as chaplain to the Queen was in the detailed advice he gave her on the Salvation Army. 'Long conversation,' he noted in his diary, 'with Queen on social matters anent Booth's scheme . . . she asked me to write down what I had said', and there follows a quite admirable five-hundred-word summing up of General Booth's aims and activities.

If technically the Royal Family were and are the parishioners of the Archbishop of Canterbury, then in many ways the Bishop of Ripon was his curate. The combined influence on the Royal Household of Davidson and Boyd Carpenter for a decade and more was profound; it was Boyd Carpenter who prepared a number of the family for Confirmation, assisted at their marriages, took part in their Coronations, ministered to them on their deathbeds and attended their funeral services. yet it was just this intimate relationship which in one respect led to difficulties, namely the Bishop's affection for the Kaiser, whom he regarded as a sincere and zealous Christian, a very able administrator and a genuine lover of peace.

King Edward VII was quick to make use of this friendship with his cousin to promote a better understanding with Germany, and in November 1902 both Kaiser and Bishop were guests at Sandringham. The King instructed the Bishop to treat in his sermon the theme of the desirability of friendship between the two nations. Boyd Carpenter duly consulted the King as to the line he should take. Arthur Balfour, the Prime Minister, and Joseph Chamberlain, then Secretary of State for the Colonies, were both present in Sandringham church on that Sunday morning, and all four congratulated the preacher on his sermon!

After that Boyd Carpenter was the Kaiser's guest on several occasions in the next ten years, the last in June 1913. There was frequent correspondence between them, the Kaiser addressing the Bishop initially as 'Dear Sir' but soon as 'My dear Bishop', and signing himself 'William I.R.'. As relations between England and Germany became increasingly strained, the

Kaiser wrote in December 1909: 'I don't dream of attacking England because I have a conscience and feel responsible to God for my acts. May you and your colleagues from the pulpit cast oil on these troubled waters, a fine work for the Church.' Again, in July 1910: 'The idea of the European churches uniting in a declaration in favour of Peace and friendly relations between the Nations is very sympathetic and congenial to me'.

The regular flow of letters each way seems to have ceased with an affectionate one from the Kaiser in January 1914; but on August 3 the Bishop penned a passionate final bid for peace: 'I can only still hope and pray that the worst form of the calamity which threatens may be averted.' The Kaiser probably never received the letter; and when the Bishop naively sent another on December 18 of the same year, Lord Stamfordham, the King's Private Secretary, declined to transmit it as breaking the law which prevented 'correspondence with the enemy'.

So ended a warm friendship which had been strongly forged by the Bishop's ministry to the Kaiser's mother at Friedrickshof in 1901: 'She gave me a seal which had been Queen Victoria's, and laid upon me one last duty – "When I am gone I want you to read the English burial service over me".' This in August 1901 the Bishop duly did, and was decorated by the Kaiser with the Prussian Royal Order of the Second Class with Star for his pastoral care of the Empress. The award expressed in tangible form the affinity which had developed between this eldest daughter of Queen Victoria and the Bishop, who represented all that was best, she felt, in the Church of England in which she had been brought up. After her death Boyd Carpenter wrote: 'She had read; she had thought; she had travelled; she had observed; she had mixed with many of the foremost minds of the time; she had taken practical part in many great and humane enterprises. Consequently her range was large, and her mental equipment was well-furnished and ready for use. Conversation with her could never become insipid; while the earnest-mindedness with which she took up a subject saved it from dwindling into pedantry . . . From the first she was full of kindness to me.'

Links also developed with the Kaiser's brother and sister-in-law, Prince Henry of Prussia and his wife Irene, the latter writing to the Bishop in January 1903: 'What I should immensely like to know is the whole organisation of the Church of England, and what [their] rights are in Parliament. Let me thank you most heartily for your latest book – please remember me to Mrs Boyd Carpenter and accept this little photo of my children and husband.' Two years later she wrote a long letter about 'my two sisters in Russia' and all their anxieties over Russia's growing unrest. One of them, Alexandra, 'cannot imagine England without beloved Grandmama. How well I remember sitting by her side, listening to your beautiful sermons – one you kindly gave me at Windsor.' The Czarina wrote to him in February 1915: 'We can only trust that this terrible war may soon come to an end – you who know all the members of our family so well can understand what we go through – relations on all sides one against the other.' Not many English people can have received letters like that in the middle of the war which tore apart the Royal Families of Europe.

All this time Boyd Carpenter was continuing with his Court Chaplaincy at home, his duties since 1903 formalised by his appointment as Clerk of the Closet to King Edward VII and from 1910 to King George V. From both he received many kindnesses, staying often at Sandringham and Windsor. With both Sovereigns there was frequent exchange of presents – a calendar, an engraving, a book – always with warm covering letters in either direction. For King Edward he drew up an interesting memorandum on the functions of the ecclesiastical members of the Royal Household, and the relation of the chaplains to the Dean of the Chapel Royal and the Clerk of the Closet. In commenting, the King's Private Secretary had to point out that the Clerk was not senior to the Dean, nor the Dean to the Clerk.

The Clerk saw King Edward for the last time at a Homage only a few days before the latter's death: 'When the formal function was over,' recorded Boyd Carpenter in his diary, 'the King addressed the new Bishop in a few sympathetic words: "You have a large diocese with a great many parishes in it, and some are not as good as they ought to be." He looked at me as he added: "We know that, don't we?" I admitted the truth. Then the King said to the newly made Bishop: "They will need a firm hand." This closed the interview. We bowed ourselves out. It was a Tuesday; on the Friday night he passed away.'

King George V made no effort to appoint a new Clerk on his accession. Over fond of the position as many must have judged Boyd Carpenter to have been, there was evidently no question of a change. He resigned the see of Ripon in 1911, no longer really robust and then in his seventieth year, but the last paragraph of his resignation letter stated firmly: 'I should like to retain my post as Clerk of the Closet in Your Majesty's Household, if Your Majesty will allow me to do so.' And retain it he did for the remaining seven years of his life.

A few months before his resignation from Ripon Boyd Carpenter had been present at the Coronation of King George V in June 1911. His account of the event survives in a letter a few days after the event: '. . . it was wonderful to think how like a dream the great reign of the great queen had gone, and the eventful reign of the late King and that the weight of Empire had fallen into younger hands, and that people had been speculating whether the great ceremony which had drawn so many thousands together was destined to be the last Coronation in English history. Yet here was the great gathering of loyal British folk . . . I had as you know to carry the

Bible – I found early in the day what a sore and grievous burden had been put upon me; when it was handed over to me together with the somewhat solid and weighty cushion, I began to ask myself whether I could carry it till the moment when I could hand it over to the Archb[isho]p. I placed it on the ground while we waited; at last the procession moved forward, and I picked up my burden . . . stepped forward, flanked by the Bishops of London and Winchester, both happier than I with the lighter burdens of paten and chalice.' The Bishop's 'muscles began to twitch, and cry out against the imposition. But I said to myself: "the matter must be seen through and there must be no failure".'

The last letter Boyd Carpenter received from the King was at the last Christmas of his life: 'My dear Bishop: I hasten to send you a line to express my best thanks for your kind letter with all its good wishes for Christmas, and for the little ash tray which you have so kindly sent me. We are indeed passing through difficult and critical times, but I feel sure that the country is sound and will rise to the occasion, and that before long we shall have a settled and honourable peace. With all good wishes for Xmas and the New Year 1918. Believe me very sincerely yours, George R.I.'.

Boyd Carpenter died nine months later. His last message to his Sovereign: 'Sir, I send you my loyal love' – summed up the spirit of ardent devotion which he felt for the Royal Family. Over the years he did a great deal to interpret the Church to the Crown and, to a lesser extent, the Crown to the Church. Despite the dangers and incongruities of his position he managed, thanks to a cultivated and balanced mind, to use every opportunity to do more than simply fulfil duties and carry out functions. Boyd Carpenter's tenure of the Clerkship, added to his already long friendship with the Royal Family, was creative and unique.

There can be no question but that HUBERT MURRAY BURGE followed the aged Boyd Carpenter because of his deep friendship with Randall Davidson. He was Davidson's trusted counsellor, a man of intellectual refinement and unaffected goodness. Here was a bishop with a gentle charm and a natural dignity who would fill the office admirably; a man in the habit of reading Browning to his ordinands on the Sunday evening after their ordination; a scholar and a saint, more at home in Oxford than in his previous see of Southwark; a man who would have found today's media pressure quite intolerable: 'People are always asking,' he once said, 'for a plain answer to a plain question, but that is the one thing so far as I can see that Christ never gave.'

Burge was that remarkable combination of classical scholar, college don, headmaster and diocesan bishop. He graduated from University College, Oxford, in 1883 and began his career as a teacher there, serving as fellow, Tutor and Dean. After eight years he was ordained priest in 1898 and three years later went to Repton for a year as Headmaster. In 1901 he moved to

Winchester where he remained, happy and successful, until 1911 when he was consecrated to be Bishop of Southwark, a reluctant recruit to the Episcopal Bench if ever there was one.

He had no parochial experience, nor was he ever fitted, either by temperament or physique, for the unremitting pressure of a diocese like Southwark, where problems were aggravated by four years of war. In letters or on visits to friends in whom he could confide, he occasionally gave vent to feelings of depression, declaring that he was not meant to be a bishop, or not fit to be one. A liberal in politics, with growing sympathies towards Labour, Burge intervened courageously, though unsuccessfully, in the 1912 Dock Strike. In the House of Lords he sponsored a measure, also unsuccessful, for the better regulation of the liquor traffic. He most definitely cared: he wanted to improve the working man's lot, but Southwark was not really his scene. The move to Oxford in 1919 saved his health, and he was a great deal more in his element among the dreaming spires and the Oxfordshire countryside than he had been living austerely in the house in Kennington, catching trams and buses on wet and foggy nights as he went about his pastoral duties south of the Thames. In the year he moved to Oxford he was made Clerk of the Closet.

Burge's correspondence with the King's Private Secretary was largely on the subject of appointments to the College of Chaplains, which under him took on its modern form. The letters reveal not only the care with which the appointments were made, but also the changed relationship between Sovereign and Clerk: from Burge's time onwards the Clerk has been very much involved in this area of work, leaving the more personal relationship with the Royal Family to others. Yet Burge had one further link with the Royal Family in his office as Chancellor of the Order of the Garter, an office in which he was followed by his successor as Clerk, Thomas Strong. He died, still Bishop of Oxford, Clerk and Chancellor, on 11 June 1925.

THOMAS BANKS STRONG was yet another member of Christ Church, Oxford, to be Clerk of the Closet. He graduated as a classicist in 1881 and was successively Lecturer, Student (1888–1901) and Dean (1901–20). He served the University as Vice-Chancellor 1913–17 and was suitably honoured as scholar, musician and administrator, receiving his DD in 1902, an honorary DMus in 1917, and being appointed GBE in 1918. In 1920 he was consecrated Bishop of Ripon, and in 1925 succeeded Burge as Bishop of Oxford, Clerk of the Closet, and Chancellor of the Order of the Garter.

This could not have been simply coincidence. Strong's work among undergraduates at Oxford during the War had been significantly recognised by his appointment as a senior member of the Order of the British Empire, and he had thus had an opportunity to meet the King. He was undoubtedly a colourful person, but he could be shy and awkward when he was making no effort to get on with people. Hating ceremonial of any kind, he refused to give it the care it occasionally demanded, his chaplain recalling that on one not untypical institution visit to a parish he had 'robed in the car (which involved a considerable wrestle with me) in order not to have to meet the assembled clergy. On arrival inside the church he was asked what hymns he would like and replied "No hymns". He got through the service at breakneck speed, escaped from the procession straight into his car, shook hands with the new incumbent, said "I hope you will be happy", and drove away.'

His time as Dean of Christ Church was a happier period than his tenure of the see – the culture of college life appealed to him much more than the episcopal minutiae which demanded his attention. 'There is one more matter, My Lord, which we ought to discuss,' said a painstaking Rural Dean, who was more than a little hurt to have the reply: 'There is nothing in heaven or earth that we have not discussed', as the Bishop rose to end the interview. Yet this abruptness concealed a spirit deeply moved by classical music (he was an accomplished pianist) and a tenderness which when some personal tragedy overtook one of his priests made him take infinite pains for his welfare. 'Religion is friendship,' he once said during an address in a poor, working-class Leeds parish. 'It is not confinement, restrictions, tied hands. It is friendship with God in and through our Lord.'

Strong's growing friendship with the King and Queen meant a very great deal to him, and Harold Anson, his biographer, recalled the immense gratitude he expressed at the kindness of Their Majesties to him personally. He often stayed with them, and always recalled his visits with great pleasure. He sometimes spoke (without any disparagement whatever) of King George V as the best type of Pass man. He felt that the King, without any great intellectual powers, did quite admirably the work which Providence had given him to do. He admired the King's grip on the Empire, his knowledge of the personalities connected with his work; and above all his very simple and devout religious life.

Strong was occasionally involved in vetting books which their authors wished to present to the King, and the Private Secretary once requested him to 'continue to refuse to forward any publications to the King unless from authors of recognised merit, and whose works are devoid of controversial matter, religious, political, social. It was indeed merciful of you to spare us any effusions from the Christian Scientists!' Strong took his office as Chancellor of the Order of the Garter seriously: every night when he went to bed he took with him the case containing the Garter jewel and ribbon. He resigned the see of Oxford and the Clerkship on 30 September 1937 and died on 8 June 1944.

CYRIL FORSTER GARBETT had a reputation for austerity and unrelenting hard work long before he was made Bishop of Winchester in 1932. He retained his selfless devotion to duty to the very last days of his life, and his journeys as Archbishop of York created a great impression wherever he went, and did the Church of England, and indeed England generally, much good.

His earlier ministry had been, for a very full twenty years, in Portsea where, unusually, he was successively curate and vicar. In 1919 he was consecrated Bishop of Southwark, a diocese which stretches from the teeming streets of south London through miles of suburbs to the pleasant pastures of Godstone deanery. He was there until 1932 when he was translated to Winchester; and ten years later to the Primacy in York.

Cyril Garbett came from a clerical family and was born in the Vicarage at Tongham near the Hog's Back. He was the eldest of five children, his father Charles being sixty when he married for the second time. His first wife had died on the voyage home from India, where he had been a chaplain in the service of the East India Company for twenty-five years. Despite a disparity in age, Charles Garbett's second marriage was a very happy one, and Cyril later became a devoted son, eventually making a home for his mother, who died during his time at Winchester. He would visit her in her part of the great house at Wolvesey five times a day with utter devotion, and was devastated by her death. Elsie, his sister, continued to run his household until his own death. Often impatient with her (lunch was at 1 o'clock, not one minute past), and indeed imperious sometimes ('get so and so to tea') he yet always went to see her before going out, and again as soon as he came in. There was a deep and abiding affection between brother and sister; he was very dependent on her, and he knew it.

The world, of course, saw none of this; only the indefatigable traveller, the House of Lords statesman, the producer of a steady stream of books and pamphlets, the preacher for the great occasion. For his enthronement sermon in York Minster he talked on the three paramount subjects he felt the Church should be tackling: evangelism, church reform and re-union. All were themes to which he returned again and again, and he was still hard at the task of communicating the Gospel in his eightieth year: 'at last,' runs the diary entry for 10 June 1954, 'my typescript has been sent to the publishers' – it was his *World Problems of Today* – 'I only hope the little book will be worth the time and trouble I have spent on it. I had no right to spend this time, but for my intense desire to show that the Church has a message on public affairs and to encourage churchmen to hear it.'

This was the man whom King George VI chose to be Clerk of the Closet in succession to Thomas Strong in 1937, and half his tenure of the office fell during the first three years of the War. Within a few weeks of its outbreak, on 24 October 1939, Garbett was at Buckingham Palace to be present at the Homage of the new bishops of London [Geoffrey Fisher] and Sheffield

[Leslie Hunter]. 'We robe in scarlet at the Palace,' he wrote in his diary; 'the bishop kneels, places his hands within the King's and repeats the oath after the Home Secretary. I then give him the Bible to kiss, which I carry on a great cushion. The King noticed the open Bible I was carrying, and asked me if at the Homage it was always open at the same place. I told him I had just asked the same question of the attendant who handed it to me in the corridor. When he said it was opened at random, I had hurriedly turned the page over, as the Bible had been open at the chapter where Job cursed the day when he was born, and I had thought this a bad omen for a new bishop! The King was greatly amused, and said it wouldn't do for a bishop to curse.' By this time Garbett had been Clerk for two years, and it seems uncharacteristic of such a meticulous man that he should not have asked the question about the Bible before.

The following summer the Clerk was back in the Palace for the Homage of the new Bishop of Leicester [Guy Vernon Smith] on 21 June 1940. 'The King looked tired but talked to us and the Home Secretary for an unusually long time. He said he had numerous letters asking for more Days of Prayer, but rightly remarked that if you are always calling people to prayer they will get to think that they need not pray unless they have a call. . . . [The King] spoke of the problems of the refugees who were pouring into England, and the difficulty of knowing what to do with them. He showed a remarkable knowledge of the industries of Leicester.'

By the time the new Bishop of St Edmundsbury and Ipswich [Richard Brook] paid Homage on 13 November 1940, Buckingham Palace had been bombed. 'Since the air raids have started, the King's rooms are on the ground floor. The corridors are cold, as the windows are still broken. As the Home Secretary was away, Sir John Anderson, now Lord President of the Council, administered the oath; he is a strong dour man, a good administrator but no parliamentarian. H.M. looked well; he has a new assurance, and is very friendly with a delightful smile. He really knows a lot about some of the social problems. We had a discussion about air raid shelters; he chaffed Anderson and said he would always be remembered for his air raid shelters if for nothing else. The King asked what could be done about the cold and damp of the surface shelters in the winter. There was an animated discussion about this. Anderson, who is always very casual, with hands in pockets, absentmindedly replied to the King's remarks: "But my dear man . . .". The King roared with laughter, turning to us with delight. Anderson hastily corrected himself, but without apology or any self-consciousness. I came away with a great consideration for the King.'

Garbett's last reference to his duties as Clerk comes in his diary after he had resigned the office: 'June 2, 1942. Bishops' War Committee in the morning. In the afternoon paid my Homage to H.M. on my translation [to York]. Herbert, the Bishop-designate of Norwich, acted as Clerk of the

Closet, and I instructed him. I have been present at the Homage of 18 bishops in 4 years'.

Thirteen years after he had handed on the office of Clerk to Percy Herbert, The Queen gave Garbett the GCVO on his eightieth birthday: 'the announcement of my Order was made over the wireless at 6.0.; I don't really know about Orders, but I understand it is the highest an ecclesiastic can have. It is not only a great compliment but a very kind action' [Diary, 6 Feb. 1955]. Cyril Garbett died on the last day of 1955.

Like several of his predecessors, PERCY MARK HERBERT had a personal link with the Royal Family before he became Clerk. He first met the King and Queen during a two-day visit to Lancashire. The tall and striking Bishop of Blackburn and his wife were invited to Knowsley Hall by the Earl and Countess of Derby, to stay the night and meet the sovereign and his consort. 'They were particularly friendly to both of us,' Herbert wrote later in a private Memoir. 'Thereafter I met the King fairly frequently, especially in Freemasonry, and I was appointed Grand Chaplain for the second time in order to act as such when the King installed the Duke of Kent as Grand Master at a most remarkable ceremony at Olympia.

'At the beginning of 1942 Garbett, Bishop of Winchester, resigned his office as Clerk of the Closet on becoming Archbishop of York, and the King asked me to succeed him. So, while still Bishop of Blackburn, though already I knew of my translation to Norwich, I became Clerk of the Closet. This was at the beginning of 1942, and at the time of writing this [1960] I still hold the office after eighteen years. This of course has meant being in fairly close and constant personal relationship with King George VI and Queen Elizabeth II.

'This is not the place to enlarge on my feelings for them, my intense and ever-increasing reverence for their characters and their devoted work, but I may rightly say that this association has been one of the most valued and valuable experiences of my life.

'For seventeen years as Bishop of Norwich I was invited to Sandringham for a week-end after Christmas, often including a day's shooting, always very happy occasions, as well as preaching there on many special occasions. The King took a special interest in my work. Thinking that this was too heavy, he took the initiative and wrote to the Lord Lieutenant asking him to raise money to provide a Suffragan Bishop, heading the list with a large donation. I have already said it was he who urged me to become Provincial Grand-Master of Freemasonry because he believed so strongly in its good influence, and thought that the position would help me in what I was trying to do in Norfolk. I may here add that he was right. I never regretted my decision, for the work brought me into close touch with hundreds of men, whom otherwise I should not have known, and helped to bridge the gulf between the Church and every-day life.'

Bishop Herbert then included his intimate recollections of a weekend spent at Sandringham at the end of December 1951 when, among other incidents, 'the King came to the Equerries' Room to speak to me about the proposed reorganisation of parishes, mostly on his estate. He entirely approved.' The other incident, little more than a month later, took Herbert to Sandringham again, this time both on his own account and on behalf of the temporarily sick Archbishop of Canterbury, to offer support to the Royal Family on the death of the King. The next day he called on Queen Mary at Marlborough House, and then reported to Lambeth Palace. In the evening he attended a meeting at St James's Palace with the Earl Marshal, securing agreement that the planned short Service in Westminster Hall should be left in the hands of the Archbishop, 'and I had some talk with Canon Venables, representing the Dean of Windsor, about the funeral service at St George's. Later I went again to Lambeth to report on these matters.' Also that day he went to the House of Lords to take his Oath of Allegiance to the new Queen.

The Coronation in 1953 was the second in which Herbert was concerned, for in 1911 he had been involved as Randall Davidson's domestic chaplain. This time, as Clerk of the Closet, he was the bearer of the specially printed and bound copy of the Bible. 'At the appropriate moment I moved from my place to hand it on its cushion to the Moderator of the Church of Scotland, standing in front of The Queen. . . . As to the service it was, I suppose, the most beautiful and best-ordered service that has ever been held. Being broadcast and televised, millions of people were able to enter it, and, if they wished, to join in its spirit and its prayers. For The Queen herself, coming at so young an age to a life-time of responsibility, it was a supreme moment of dedication. I know how deeply she appreciated its religious character.'

Bishop Herbert continued as Clerk for another ten years after the Coronation, and was present at a total of 75 Homages during his 21 years in office. For the last four of those years he no longer held the see of Norwich, but had somehow come to assume that his successor in that diocese, Launcelot Fleming, would succeed him as Clerk. During the summer of 1963 he said as much to Fleming, and was rather embarrassed when he discovered this was not the Sovereign's intention.

In his retirement Herbert lived in a grace-and-favour house in the Great Park at Windsor and – the old man's prerogative – became increasingly vague. He took services in the Park chapel from time to time when the chaplain was away and, on one occasion taking Matins for the first time in decades (bishops in office celebrate Holy Communion every Sunday but rarely lead Matins in public), he used his own prayer book for the State Prayers, and fell straight into the trap of using an uncorrected prayer for the Royal Family. So he prayed 'for Alexandra the Queen Mother (she had

been dead for thirty-five years) . . . (pause) . . . What's the boy's name?
. . . (mumble, mumble) . . . and all the Royal Family.' Herbert died in
January 1968, and thus passed a giant of a man, the longest serving Clerk
since Henry Philpott, and to many in the Church of England the man who
personally and uniquely symbolised the close link between the Crown and
the Established Church.

NOTES

Biographies based on: H.D.A. Major, *The Life and Letters of William Boyd Carpenter* (1925); *Discourses and Letters of Hubert Murray Burge*, edited with a Memoir by Lord Charnwood (1930); Harold Anson, *T.B. Strong: Bishop, musician, Dean, Vice-Chancellor* (1949); Charles Smyth; *Cyril Forster Garbett, Archbishop of York* (1959); MS. Autobiographical Memoir by Percy Herbert, in possession of his son Mr David Herbert; *Crockford's Clerical Directory*.

1. Bell, G.K.A., *Randall Davidson*, 56, 64.
2. Aspinall, A., (ed.), *The Later Correspondence of George III*, (1962), i. 183.

CHAPTER NINE

A New Generation

T HE END OF the long and intimate service of Percy Herbert was the end of an era. He knew the members of the Royal Family almost as well as Boyd Carpenter had done, if not for so long. After him there was no bishop on the Bench who could claim such knowledge on appointment, and also none who could possibly take such time as they had done from the demands now made upon a bishop. This is not to suggest that Herbert's successors have in any way seen the office of Clerk of the Closet as of little importance. Indeed, all have valued very highly the close link with the sovereign which the Clerk enjoys.

In accepting the offer of the Clerkship in 1903 Bishop Boyd Carpenter told the King's Private Secretary: 'I trust that in this honourable office I may be able to render some real service to the King.'[1] His trust was amply fulfilled. On his retirement in 1937 his successor but one, Bishop Strong, outlined his perception of the duties he was about to relinquish. For him there were four functions – preaching at St James's on the Second Sunday in Lent, presenting bishops at Homages, suggesting names for the College of Chaplains, and recommending (or otherwise) the acceptance of books ('The books that have been sent to me have been really bad ones and I have never recommended the acceptance of any of them.'). Later in that same month the King's Private Secretary assured Bishop Garbett, then prospective Clerk, that the duties of the office were 'in no way arduous'.[2] On his resignation five years later Garbett declared that he had found the post 'full of interest'. The preaching role has changed since Strong's day, but the other duties remain firmly attached to the Clerkship.

When asked how he came to be appointed Clerk, ROGER PLUMPTON WILSON remembered the Prime Minister's Ecclesiastical Secretary 'nosing about' when he was still Vicar of Holy Trinity, South Shore in Blackpool.

'That was more likely to see if I would be right for Wakefield rather than right for the Closet,' he mused. Certainly, he was invited to Sandringham while he was Bishop of Wakefield and 'that was probably for vetting'. 'I would imagine,' Wilson said, 'I was put up by Percy Herbert,' who had been Wilson's diocesan at Blackburn and who had appointed him to Holy Trinity in 1939. 'I expect the Archbishop was consulted. I know when the time came for me to give up the office, I suggested Gordon Fallows to the Palace, and that went to Lambeth for approval. Certainly my impression,' Wilson concluded, 'is that the appointment is a very personal one, made directly by the Sovereign through her Private Secretary talking the matter over with very few people, and simply seeking the Archbishop of Canterbury's approval.'[3]

Roger Wilson, a product of Keble College, Oxford, and Westcott House, Cambridge, held curacies in Liverpool and London and then spent most of the war years in Blackpool (1939–44), moving to Southwell diocese as Archdeacon of Nottingham (1944–9). In 1949 he was consecrated to be Bishop of Wakefield, and in 1958 he was translated to the see of Chichester.

'A natural modesty, combined with splendid looks and bearing,' writes Bishop Simon Phipps, 'made Roger Wilson an exceptionally attractive figure. He looked the part on every occasion, towering over those around him, yet with never a hint of the pompous, but rather of the pure in heart. Although he was an active bishop for some twenty-five years, he never failed to carry with him the quickly sensitive compassion of the faithful parish priest. He was not a prophet nor an innovator; he just watched quietly and perceptively over the churches in his care, presiding over a supportive diocesan administration, loyally implementing policies agreed in assembly or synod, and giving endless and usually unseen attention to the personal needs of clergy and laity as they came his way. All this generated a widespread atmosphere of respect for his integrity and affection for his character.'

Early in Roger Wilson's Clerkship the rule for the retirement of chaplains at 70 was introduced, and every new chaplain was informed of the rule on appointment. There was also a comparatively rare example of the Clerk vetting books which their authors wished to give to the Sovereign. On 5 May 1966 an Anglican priest made a case to The Queen's Private Secretary for two books by a German Roman Catholic lady. The Private Secretary sent the books to the Clerk. He consulted a German-speaking priest who translated one of them for him. Dr Wilson concluded that while the books, which consisted of short devotional studies on Christian unity and had a deeply spiritual content, denoted Roman forms of piety, they were 'sound and healthy', and he could 'see no objection to Her Majesty accepting them'. Her Majesty did so, and thus the Clerk of the Closet had carried out one of his less common duties.

In March 1974 Wilson wrote to The Queen to say that 'it was right' that as he was resigning from the see of Chichester in the following month he should tender his resignation as Clerk of the Closet. 'The office,' he declared, 'ought in my humble opinion to be surrendered by me when I cease to hold official diocesan responsibilities, and therefore I hope you will accept my request to resign at your convenience on or after the date of my retirement from the see.' Martin Charteris, later Lord Charteris of Amisfield, The Queen's Private Secretary, replied by return: 'Her Majesty accepts with much regret that it would probably be right for you to resign as Clerk of the Closet more or less at the same time as you give up your diocesan responsibilities.' Then he virtually contradicts that statement: 'As you will know Percy Herbert retained the appointment of Clerk of the Closet for some time after he left Norwich, so I do not believe there is any need for your resignation to become effective at exactly the same time as your retirement from the see.' The Private Secretary must also have known that Philpott and Boyd Carpenter had also stayed in office after leaving their sees. Wilson and Charteris, despite meeting at Buckingham Palace in April to discuss 'who might be appointed', seem to have reached no conclusion; there was evidently correspondence in December when Wilson must have been asked to continue in office until May, for on 17 July 1975 Charteris reopened the matter: 'You were good enough to say before Christmas that you were ready to continue in office until The Queen returned from Japan in May. This you have nobly done; indeed you have done more than you promised as it is now July!

'Her Majesty is most grateful to you. She believes with regret that the time has now come for her to accept your resignation, and I am therefore on her instructions writing to the Bishop of Sheffield [Gordon Fallows] to offer him the succession of your office. If he accepts, I suggest that the changeover should actually take place at the end of October after The Queen returns from Nigeria.' And Charteris adds in his own hand: 'I do not believe it could be effected before, and I (hope) you will not mind doing one more homage.'[4] Bishop Wilson, made KCVO in July 1974, eventually resigned on 31 October 1975, and went to live in Wrington near Bristol, where he soon began to exercise a quietly effective retirement ministry, greatly loved as ever.

Roger Wilson suggested the name of WILLIAM GORDON FALLOWS, a former Chaplain to The Queen, expressly because, as Bishop of Sheffield, he served in the Northern Province. Charteris' letter to Wilson just quoted clearly indicates that they had agreed on a successor before the end of 1974, that The Queen had approved of the suggestion, but that Bishop Fallows had not been (at least officially) approached. By 25 July he had agreed and the Comptroller, Lt.-Col. (later Sir Eric) Penn, had written to him with a draft announcement of the appointment.

Gordon Fallows was ordained in 1937 after St Edmund Hall and Ripon Hall, Oxford. A curacy at Leamington Spa was followed by service in the parish of Styvechale, Coventry, throughout the war years, and then the influential vicarage of Preston (Lancs.). Between 1955 and 1959 he combined that with the Archdeaconry of Lancaster. In 1959 he was appointed Principal of Ripon Hall, Oxford, where he stayed until he was consecrated as Bishop of Pontefract in 1968. In 1971 he was translated to Sheffield. He died on 17 August 1979.

Gordon Fallows was a distinguished Principal of his old theological college, Ripon Hall. Dr F.W. Dillistone remembers him as 'a gracious host, giving wise leadership to his students, extending the Hall's buildings and maintaining links with the University. It was obvious that in course of time he would be appointed to a bishopric, but the first move was not to a diocese but to the suffragan bishopric of Pontefract in Wakefield diocese. The title was entirely relevant, for in contrast to the broken bridge which gave the town its name, Gordon was a bridge builder, first in Wakefield and later in Sheffield. In far from easy circumstances his sympathetic understanding and wonderful gift of humour broke down barriers wherever they existed.

'His association with Eric Treacy the Bishop of Wakefield could hardly have been happier, but a far more demanding task awaited him. In a comparatively short time he was nominated to become Bishop of Sheffield. It was a great industrial area, but new technologies were already leading to unsettlement and problems in labour relations. Gordon had to build up a team of supporters and to win the confidence of conflicting interests in the diocese.

'This he gradually did with outstanding success. He knew a great deal about the history of the Modern Churchman's Union and its leading personalities, but he never allowed this to come in the way of his own constructive and balanced outlook. He was quick to recognize important new developments, but his heart was set on building up a strong Christian witness in Sheffield which would embrace any sectional interests.'

In December 1972 Gordon was chosen to chair the House of Bishops' working group on the Deployment of the Clergy, and there followed eighteen months of careful and detailed work by the eight-member group culminating in the production of what quickly became known as the Sheffield Report. A member of the group when Bishop of Warrington here bears witness to the able and sensitive guidance of its chairman in what proved to be both a radical and a universally accepted method by which the clergy of the Church of England were to be deployed to the best advantage.

'The choice of Gordon to be Clerk of the Closet was probably quite unexpected,' Dr Dillistone recalls, 'but the source to him of very great pleasure. The journeys to the Palace and the privileged meetings with The

Queen were in marked contrast to the often grim conditions of the industrial North.

[His wife] Edna had made the Bishop's home and garden outstandingly beautiful through her gardening skill and the children seemed well established. Then came a series of shattering experiences: the illness and death of his daughter, followed by his own terminal illness, which he bore wih heroic courage. The response to his selfless labours gained full recognition at the great Memorial Service in the Cathedral. Sheffield and the wider diocese recognized that they had lost a leader who, entirely natural and approachable, was also decisive, with eyes set on the future. In the best sense he was liberal and open-hearted, a bridge-builder in Oxford, in Pontefract and finally in Sheffield.'

'I look forward,' Gordon Fallows had written to the new Bishop of Bath and Wells, in November 1975, 'to having the pleasure of being your prop forward on the occasion of your Homage to Her Majesty The Queen at 12.30 p.m. on Friday 12th December 1975. I enclose the notes bequeathed to me by my predecessor as Clerk of the Closet. It is a simple ceremony and we can have a few words about it when we robe together at the Palace. . . . All best wishes for the move . . . .' Four years later the phone rang at the Palace in Wells. It was The Queen's Private Secretary, then Sir Philip Moore, wondering whether that same Bishop would accept an invitation from Her Majesty to follow Bishop Fallows and become the next Clerk of the Closet.

So the tenth member of Christ Church, Oxford, and the first Bishop of Bath and Wells duly received the royal Warrant, signed and stamped by the Lord Chamberlain, then Lord Maclean of Duart, to certify that 'The Right Reverend JOHN MONIER BICKERSTETH, MA, Bishop of Bath and Wells, is by the Queen's Command hereby appointed into the Place and Quality of Clerk of the Closet to Her Majesty to have, hold, exercise and enjoy the said Place, together with all Rights, Profits, Privileges and Advantages thereunto belonging. This appointment to be during Her Majesty's pleasure and to become void on the death of the Sovereign.'

A private audience followed a few days later in Her Majesty's sitting-room at Buckingham Palace, and what was to be two months short of ten years in the Royal Household had begun. Some weeks later Peter Nott, then Suffragan Bishop of Taunton and now Bishop of Norwich, wrote about the appointment in the *Bath and Wells Diocesan News*, congratulating his Diocesan on the honour, with the kind and unexceptionable comment (which no one could confirm or deny): 'His background in the ordained ministry has obviously fitted him for the job.' Nearly six years' Army service at home, in Normandy and in India led via Oxford and Wells Theological College to ordination in 1950 – the fifth generation of Bickersteth clergymen since 1821 – and then four memorable years under

Mervyn Stockwood in Bristol. There followed two eight-year incum-
bencies, at St John's, Hurst Green, near Oxted and at St Stephen's,
Chatham, and then an invitation to be Suffragan Bishop of Warrington
under Bishop Stuart Blanch of Liverpool, a very real return to Bickersteth
roots in Lancashire. The work was immensely congenial under such a
gifted diocesan, and included exciting ecumenical enterprises and leadership of a lively industrial chaplaincy.

A letter from the Prime Minister in July 1975 relayed The Queen's offer
of the historic see of Bath and Wells, and so began a twelve-year
occupation of what Pevsner described as 'without doubt the most
memorable of all Bishop's palaces in England' and a see with around 330
parishes. To travel within the diocese were added visits on church business
to Russia, Australia, Sri Lanka, Central Africa, Romania and the United
States; and a shorter, and never-to-be-forgotten, journey for a weekend at
Sandringham to shoot and preach (in that chronological order) when the
King and Queen of Spain were also guests.

Resignation from Bath and Wells in 1987 was so timed to enable a
successor to take office in time to attend the Lambeth Conference which
was due the following summer. The Clerkship, however, has since Bishop
Philpott's time often been retained after retirement, and a two-year period
was agreed upon, after which the lack of attendance at Bishops' Meetings
and the General Synod would inevitably mean a lessening of contacts with
the leaders of the Church; and knowing whom to nominate as new
Chaplains to The Queen would become more difficult.

Bishop Strong had put the duty of preaching at St James's on the second
Sunday in Lent each year as the first of the duties of the Clerk's office,[5] a
survival from the days when Clerks frequently preached before the
Sovereign in one of the royal establishments. Inheriting the tradition of the
Lent preachment, the new Clerk and Deputy Clerk between them decided
in 1980 that this fixed date was an unnecessary and restricting custom. So,
for the last decade the Sub-Dean of the Chapel Royal begins every
September to fill his rota for the following year by consulting the Dean (the
Bishop of London) on a convenient date for him, the Deputy Clerk does the
same for the Clerk, and the Sub-Almoner does the same for the Almoner,
the third bishop in the Ecclesiastical Household. Thus the three bishops,
whose diaries are likely to be much fuller than those of the chaplains, move
happily round the calendar, sometimes preaching at the monthly Eucharist,
and each year varying the Church season when they appear. The three
bishops as Dean, Almoner and Clerk all rank *pari passu* within the
Household, and what might seem a complicated system is made quite
simple because the Deputy Clerk, the Sub-Dean and the Sub-Almoner are
one and the same person – for these ten years Canon Anthony Caesar.

For the new Clerk, the first preachment on appointment was particularly moving because of childhood memories. Fifty years before he had been a regular, albeit very juvenile, worshipper. With a home in London and the secretary of the Jerusalem and the East Mission for a father, his musical mother brought their young children to sit in one of the small box pews on decani side Sunday by Sunday through the second half of the 1920s, to imbibe something of the great traditions of Byrd and Purcell. Certainly the fine speaking voice of Canon Percival, then the Sub-Dean, made a lasting impression, though more typical of a young child's memories is the musty, dusty smell of the large red hassocks, still remembered by the Bishop of Bath and Wells on his first return visit in 1980. The congregation that day seemed to like this childhood recollection in the sermon.

The second task of the Clerk is to approve, or disapprove, of any book on an ecclesiastical subject which its author wishes to present to the Sovereign. The origin of this role has not been established, but the Clerk has to some extent succeeded the Confessor of medieval and Tudor monarchs, and it was obviously essential, in order to maintain the position of the Crown at the head of the Established Church after the Reformation, that no publication likely to corrupt the Protestant soul of the Supreme Head of the Church of England should come before royal eyes. There have not been many occasions for the responsibility to be exercised by the Clerk in the last ten years, but an able church historian was warmly encouraged to present his *magnum opus* to The Queen; an American woman, however, who had written some pamphlets on clairvoyancy which she thought the 'Queen of England' ought to possess received a very firm refusal.

Undoubtedly the highlight of the decade in this particular role was the unique experience of the Clerk in taking Her Majesty through the salient features of the *Alternative Service Book*. A private audience was granted in the Spring of 1980 at which The Queen and Clerk went over together the ten or twelve points which the Clerk had prepared beforehand at the request of the Private Secretary. Whether or not this first official alternative to the Book of Common Prayer in two hundred years would pass the criterion envisaged by those who introduced the Act of Supremacy must remain one of the imponderables of History. Certainly there had been a remarkable convergence of both Catholic and Evangelical thinking in the final approval stage at General Synod level, and a comfortable passage through Parliament ensued.

There was an interesting discussion that morning in Her Majesty's private apartments, and an amusing side to the public presentation at the ensuing General Synod session. 'We had thought,' said the Archbishop of York, Dr Stuart Blanch, in that delightfully throw-away style for which he was famous, 'to give Your Majesty a pair of handsomely bound volumes, one containing the Book of Common Prayer (1662) and one the Alternative Service Book (1980). But then we decided that that was a rather extravagant idea, as you almost certainly would already have several copies of the familiar book. So here is . . .', and the rest of his remarks were drowned in tumultuous laughter and applause in which The Queen wholeheartedly joined, as the single special copy was handed over.

The Clerk's third duty, to guide new diocesan bishops through their Homage to the Sovereign, has been exercised thirty-seven times in the past ten years. This simple and significant ceremony brings the Secretary of State for Home Affairs and the Clerk to Buckingham Palace every three or four months. Three Home Secretaries have held office during the decade – William Whitelaw, Leon Brittan and Douglas Hurd. Mr (now Sir Leon) Brittan felt that, as a Jew, he should not administer a Trinitarian oath, so he usually asked Lord Whitelaw to stand in for him. Mr Peter Walker stood in once, when the Bishop of Worcester took the oath, as the bishop's home is in his constituency; he had performed the same duty for the previous Bishop some years earlier. Four sees have been vacant twice in the last decade – Blackburn, Bradford, Southwell and Sodor and Man – and all five senior sees, Canterbury, York, London, Durham and Winchester have changed hands.

A date having been fixed some weeks earlier, the Clerk welcomes the new Bishop to the Palace half an hour before the audience time. They robe together in the billiard room off the entrance hall and the Master of the Household then takes them through to the Bow Room where they meet the members of the Household on duty, usually the Private Secretary, the Equerry and the Lady-in-Waiting. The Home Secretary joins the contingent and, after The Queen's bell rings, goes into the 1844 room on his own for a few minutes with Her Majesty. When the bell rings a second time, the doors of the 1844 room are thrown open again, and the Master of the Household announces: 'The Bishop of ——, Your Majesty.' Bishop and Clerk then step forward, The Queen shakes the new Bishop by the hand, goes to her chair in the window and sits down. The new Bishop kneels at the faldstool in front of Her Majesty and puts his hands together. The Queen clasps them, and the Home Secretary, standing on her right, begins to recite the Oath, section by section, the new Bishop repeating each sonorous phrase after him. The Clerk, who has been standing on the new Bishop's right, holds before him a cushion with the open Coronation Bible resting on it. After the final words, which are 'God Save Queen Elizabeth' the Bishop kisses the Bible. The Queen and the Bishop rise, the Clerk puts cushion and Bible on a nearby table, and The Queen begins a short conversation with the three men. The only variation in the arrangements is that for the Homage of an Archbishop, the Clerk and the Archbishop robe in the bedroom suite reserved for visiting heads of state!

From Easter 1989 onwards, instead of a rather battered copy of the Scriptures which had belonged to a nineteenth-century Lord Chamberlain, the Bible used has been a replica of the Authorised Version specially bound for the present Queen's Coronation. The actual one used in the Coronation service belongs to the Lambeth Palace Library; the one used at Homages belongs to the Royal Library at Windsor and is now brought up to London for each Homage. The Clerk has for some years chosen at what page to open it, seeking to fit the text to the man.

The fourth role of the Clerk is as Head of the College of Chaplains, where he exercises a crucial role in the appointment of the men who are made Chaplains to The Queen. There are thirty-six of them on the Rota of Waits who take their annual turn at preaching either in the Chapel Royal at St James's (in the winter months) or in the Queen's Chapel, Marlborough House (from Easter until October). Other annual preachers there are, by tradition, the Clerk himself as Head of the College, the Almoner, the Dean of the Chapel Royal (the Bishop of London for the time being), and the Deans of Windsor and Westminster. Visitors are always welcome and there is generally a congregation of a hundred or more, glad to revel in the superb singing and setting.

As Head of the College of Chaplains the Clerk and his wife were invited to join the congregation which in two successive years filled St Paul's Cathedral for Royal occasions. The first was the Thanksgiving service on 15 July 1980 in commemoration of the 80th birthday of Queen Elizabeth the Queen Mother. Dr Runcie preached an unusual and memorable sermon, his subject being the face of this greatly-loved person. The following summer came the invitation for 29 July to attend the marriage of Prince Charles to Lady Diana Spencer. The Household party coming in a coach from St James's Palace was nearly late for the service because of the traffic jams, but enjoyed the cheers of the excited crowds along Fleet Street and up Ludgate Hill, past the troops lining the route and the office workers cheering from every available window.

The Clerk also twice represented The Queen at Memorial Services. The first was for the Dean of Westminster, Eric Abbott. Edward Carpenter, soon himself to be Dean, received The Queen's Representative as he alighted from the royal car (entered a few streets away in Smith Square) and escorted him up the nave to the stall in the Quire. The other occasion was at The Queen's Chapel of the Savoy in memory of Canon Edwyn Young, the retired Chaplain of the Royal Victorian Order and for long a member of the College of Chaplains. As he was also an old friend, this was a particular privilege. On this occasion the royal car was not at the appointed place at the appointed time, but resort to a taxi at almost the last minute just averted a crisis.

Far away from the London scene, the Clerk was on Anglican Communion business, representing the Archbishop of Canterbury in two Commonwealth countries during 1984 and The Queen gladly agreed to his tentative suggestion beforehand that messages of goodwill from Her

Majesty might be conveyed by him. So at the consecration of Bishop Andrew Kumarage in Kurunegala, Sri Lanka, the Clerk read greetings from The Queen; and again, at the centenary celebrations of the huge diocese of Riverina, New South Wales. In both countries the Clerk of the Closet and his wife received immensely affectionate welcomes, and delighted gratitude was expressed that someone from The Queen's Ecclesiastical Household should have brought a special word for them from the Head of the Church of England.

There was one other remarkable church occasion, the Thanksgiving Service in commemoration of The Queen's sixtieth birthday, held on a rainy morning at St George's Chapel, Windsor, on 21 April 1986. The Queen decided to entrust the conduct of the service to the Dean of Windsor and the Clerk. The latter read the prayers for The Queen and the Royal Family, and at the end gave the blessing, in the presence of both Archbishops. It was, by Her Majesty's own choice, the one used at her wedding: 'God the Father, God the Son, and God the Holy Spirit bless, preserve and keep you; the Lord mercifully with his favour look upon you, and so fill you with all spiritual benediction and grace that you may so live in this life that in the world to come you may have life everlasting.' It was very moving indeed for the Clerk to look down from the High Altar towards this utterly dedicated person in her stall, surrounded by her Garter knights.

Twelve hours after the service was over an interior-lit royal car passed along the Mall. It was nearly midnight. A handful of bystanders was still there to clap the still-smiling Queen on a day when the enormous regard and affection in which Her Majesty is held had been amply demonstrated by the cheering crowds in the rain at Windsor, by the 6,000 children who had danced along the Mall to the Palace forecourt that afternoon, waving 120,000 daffodils, and by the distinguished audience at the evening's Royal Performance at Covent Garden. 'You see,' said a Chinese official to one of the equerries during Her Majesty's first state visit to China later that year, 'it is wonderful to know now the lady who is head of the whole world outside China.' Her sometime Clerk echoes the sentiment, having been privileged to lead the Chaplains to the Queen in prayer for Her Majesty during the 1980's, as she has moved faithfully and tirelessly about the nation, the Commonwealth and indeed, as that unknown Chinaman ingenuously remarked, the world itself.

NOTES

1. Windsor, Royal Archives, W 37/24.
2. Ibid., Geo. VI/2346 (letter 20 Sept. 1937).
3. Letter from Bishop Wilson to Bishop Bickersteth.
4. Windsor, Royal Archives, Geo. VI/2346 (letter 13 Sept. 1937).

CHAPTER TEN

PRESTES FYNDING: THE CLERKS AND THE ROYAL CHAPLAINS

T HE MOST INFLUENTIAL, although at the same time perhaps the least well-known work done by the Clerk of the Closet has developed within the last eighty years or so, and has only come to its full significance from the time when Hubert Burge was Clerk in the 1920s. This is the Clerk's role as adviser to the Sovereign in the appointment of Royal Chaplains, and his headship of the College of Chaplains in consequence. Yet it is possible to see that Clerks in the sixteenth century were also intimately involved with the chaplains who served the Tudor monarchs, the direct ancestors of today's Chaplains to The Queen.

By the beginning of the sixteenth century the Clerk of the Closet had two roles within the Royal Household quite independent of his duty to furnish the King's Closet. One duty, which was not formally enshrined in Edward IV's time but which was regularly carried out by Peter Greves for King Henry VII and by several Clerks for King Henry VIII, was to pay a number of Mass priests 'whiche singeth for the Kinges grace in divers places . . .'. John Heron, Treasurer of Henry VII's Household, recorded these and other payments such as gifts to preachers, to the gentlemen and children of the Chapel Royal, and to the King's Confessor. The sum to the priests varied slightly each year, but in October 1505 amounted to £35 12s. 6d. for a half year, paid in arrears.[1] Henry VIII's Clerks in the late 1520s provided wax for candles for the shrines of King Henry VI at Windsor and Our

Lady of Pew at Doncaster, and still in 1539 paid the wages of priests singing at those two shrines and at St Edward's shrine at Westminster Abbey and King Henry VI's at Eton. By 1546 four poor priests were being supported – at Windsor, Eton, Westminster Abbey and St Stephen's Chapel.[2] The end of the chantries put an end to this particular responsibility.

By that time, however, successive Clerks had established themselves in a second role, at the heart of part of the Royal Household which was quite independent of both the Chapel Royal and the Closet. The Household Ordinance of 1478[3] laid upon the Clerk of the Closet the duty of 'warning' such chaplains 'as likith the King or the chambrelayne to attend to do service any day or wyke to the King'. The body of royal chaplains was, under this Ordinance, to be organised to attend the Sovereign on a regular basis, with the Clerk acting as a messenger, conveying the wishes of the King or the Chamberlain of the Household to the chaplains. This link between the royal chaplains and the Clerk of the Closet continued throughout the sixteenth century, and was revived in the twentieth when the Clerk of the Closet was for the first time placed at the head of a formally constituted College of Chaplains.

At the time of the 1478 Ordinance, the King's chaplains formed a most distinguished body of men, including Christopher Urswick, later to be Royal Almoner, John Gunthorpe, civil servant and later Dean of Wells, and John Bailly, diplomat and Dean of St George's, Windsor.[4] At the funeral of King Henry VII in 1509, when twelve chaplains were listed together, they were linked with 'Peter of the Closet', Peter Greves, whose connection with the royal chaplains was thus confirmed. These twelve were, again, men of importance: Thomas Hobbys, Dean of Windsor and a Master in Chancery; William Lichfield, canon of St Stephen's, Westminster, and Dean of Tamworth; Robert Honywood, a lawyer who held a canonry at Windsor and the archdeaconry of Taunton; Richard Hatton, diplomat and Provost of King's College, Cambridge; John Esterfield, canon of Windsor and theologian; Reginald West, brother of the courtier Lord de la Warr and Sub-Dean of Wells; and a young man yet to make his mark, Thomas Wolsey.[5]

As a matter of course, therefore, the Clerk accompanied the twelve royal chaplains whom Henry VIII took with him to the Field of Cloth of Gold in 1520, including the Master of the Rolls, Richard Pace the Secretary, Richard Rawlins the Almoner, and the Dean of the Chapel Royal, together described as 'concellors spirituall'. The rest included John Longland, Dean of Salisbury and soon to be Bishop of Lincoln; John Clerk, an able diplomat and shortly afterwards Bishop of Bath and Wells; and William Knight, lawyer, diplomat, and Clerk's successor at Wells.[6] Men like these were the 'chaplains of dignity' who attended the christening of Prince

Edward in 1537,[7] the men who sat at table with the first and second Masters of the Household, just above the third and fourth Masters and the Clerk of the Closet.[8]

John Rudde, Henry VIII's last Clerk, accompanied the royal chaplains at their master's obsequies in 1547 – a group of seven men including John Redman, the first Master of Trinity College, Cambridge, Richard Cox, tutor to Prince Edward the later Bishop of Ely, Owen Oglethorpe, later Bishop of Carlisle, who crowned Queen Elizabeth in 1559 but who was deprived for refusing her the oath of allegiance, and Nicholas Ridley, who with Latimer and Cranmer faced Oglethorpe, among others, in that famous disputation at Oxford in 1554.[9]

Some of these men were, perhaps, too conservative for the new régime, and the young Edward VI was accompanied at his coronation by five new chaplains, including Anthony Otway and John Lele or Lelewe, a Frenchman who had served Henry VIII as 'planter of grafts' and maker and deviser of the King's arbours. He was now described as 'maker of herbore'.[10] No Clerk seems to have been present on that occasion, but only a few years later, at the young King's burial, two chaplains, Otway and Edmund Grindal (later Queen Elizabeth's second Archbishop of Canterbury), walked together in procession with those who had been in constant attendance on the late King; and five others were listed together, with Mr Latimer at the head and Mr Rudde at the foot. Mr Rudde was, of course, Henry VIII's old Clerk who had been kept in office and was still serving closely with the royal chaplains.[11]

Otway and Grindal were in a special position at the time of the King's death because of a new arrangement. The government, concerned to promote the Reformed doctrines in the country through select and able preachers, established a group of royal chaplains, two of whom would at any time be in attendance on the King while the rest were away preaching. Grindal, reformist preacher extraordinary, was among those concerned to assess preachers' suitability and was inevitably himself chosen.[12]

It seems unlikely that the pattern of preachers outlived the King, but the twelve chaplains were maintained by Queen Mary, and at her funeral in 1558 they were described as 'Ordinary Chaplains of the Closet', a title which clearly establishes the link between chaplains and Closet. Given the traditional allowance of cloth for their appearance at the Queen's obsequies, they are listed among the records of the Lord Chamberlain in company with the Clerk of the Closet, Mr Thurlande. After them are the staff of the Chapel Royal, including Archdeacon Carew, Dean of the Chapel, and among the twenty-four gentlemen Thomas Tallis, the composer, and Robert Bassocke, the Sergeant of the Vestry, both of whom had served in the Chapel Royal in Edward VI's time and were to serve Queen Elizabeth.[13]

Mourning cloth for Queen Elizabeth's funeral in 1603 was issued to a large number of clergymen, but the basic pattern of chaplains and Chapel Royal was still retained. The list is headed by seven bishops, the Almoner and Sub-Almoner, and fifteen chaplains including John Thornborough, Clerk of the Closet. After them come the Dean and Prebendaries of Westminster and the staff of the Chapel Royal.[14] The clerical establishment of the Household was considerably enlarged under James I. The King, the Queen and the Prince of Wales each had a staff of clergymen: the Prince's comprised a confessor, an almoner, sixteen chaplains, three gentlemen and twelve children for his chapel, together with a clerk and groom for his closet and two yeomen for his vestry. All these were present at his funeral in 1612.[15] The Queen's clerical establishment at her death in 1619 comprised an almoner, eighteen chaplains (including her Dutch chaplain) and a clerk for her closet.[16]

Eight of the King's own chaplains were present at Queen Anne's funeral, including Dr Curle, later Bishop of Bath and Wells, and the full complement of the Chapel Royal – the Sub-Dean, eight ministers, the Master of the Children and the Clerk of the Cheque; twenty-two gentlemen including Orlando Gibbons, one of the organists, the Sergeant of the Vestry and twelve children.[17] Six years later, at the King's own funeral, the Chapel staff included Thomas Tompkins the organist, Orlando Gibbons the privy organist, Richard Griffith the organ blower, and John Stephens, recorder of songs, the whole totalling fifty-nine people. The royal chaplains, who included among their number eight deans and the Archdeacon of London, numbered seventy.[18]

Less than twenty years later, during the period 1641–4, the Household of Charles I included among its number a list of chaplains even longer than that of his father. The total who served during that period was one hundred and seventy, but a distinction of importance was then made: forty-seven were described simply as chaplains, the rest were 'chaplains extraordinary'. The first group included ten deans, all men of considerable influence in the Church in the opening years of the Civil War; men who, like Dean Walter Raleigh of Wells, were to suffer for their adherence to the sovereign they had served in person and the Church to which they owed allegiance.[19] These were the men who, four each month, were in constant attendance on the Sovereign, the 'chaplains in waiting' who constituted a regular part of the Royal Household for the next two centuries and more.[20]

The 'chaplains in waiting' or 'chaplains of the month' naturally had seats in the Chapel Royal, and ranked beside the Clerk of the Council, the Clerk of the Signet, and the Clerk of the Privy Council.[21] By the early years of the eighteenth century, and probably much earlier, their duties included saying prayers twice a day in the Private Oratory, and also saying grace if the Clerk of the Closet should not be present.[22] By the early nineteenth century the Ecclesiastical Household also included ten Priests in Ordinary, two Reading Chaplains at Whitehall Chapel, a Chaplain, Reader and Preacher at Hampton Court, a Household Chaplain at Kensington Palace, and a Reader at Windsor.[23] Evidently not to be outdone, the Prince Regent increased his Ecclesiastical Household from a Clerk of the Closet, a Household Chaplain and thirty-nine Clerks in Ordinary in 1806 to an establishment headed by Frederick William Blomberg, probably his own half-brother, as Clerk of the Closet, a Household Chaplain who was also his Librarian, a Private Chaplain, and eighty-seven Chaplains in Ordinary in 1810.[24]

In 1860 the Chapel Royal Commissioners considered that the number of chaplains might be reduced to thirty-six, but that their duties should remain unchanged: to preach in the Chapel Royal, to be ready to officiate in the private chapel at Buckingham Palace, and to assist in the Chapel Royal at St James's. Nine Honorary Chaplains were appointed in 1862 as the number of Chaplains in Ordinary was reduced to thirty-nine, their duties including preaching on the fifth Sunday in any month.[25] By 1894 the number of Chaplains in Ordinary had been reduced to thirty-seven and the Honorary Chaplains correspondingly increased to make the traditional total of forty-eight.[26]

The College of Chaplains

In 1906 Dr Boyd Carpenter, then Clerk of the Closet, submitted to King Edward VII a memorandum as follows: 'The Clerk of the Closet then is a Prelate who becomes chief Chaplain to the King. He is, if I may use the words, head of the College of Chaplains'. When sending a copy to Lord Stamfordham, the King's Private Secretary, the Bishop noted that it had been approved by the King. The King had also intimated that instead of the 'embroidered scarf' worn by all the Chaplains and the Clerk, he wished the Clerk to wear a brooch or badge to obviate 'the Royal Crown and Cypher occupying a position usually reserved for some sacred emblem'.[27]

In 1911, after a meeting with Lord Stamfordham to discuss the question of chaplains, the Clerk sent him a summary of the discussion: first, that the college should for the future consist of the Clerk, two or three Deputy Clerks, twelve Chaplains in Ordinary, and twenty-four Honorary Chaplains; second, that new Deputies would be chosen from among the Chaplains in Ordinary unless His Majesty should choose otherwise; and that the senior Honorary Chaplain should succeed to the vacancy as a Chaplain in Ordinary; and thirdly 'that the duty of recommending names of Clergymen or Chaplains for appointment should rest with the Clerk of the Closet . . .'. Thus the number of forty-eight chaplains, four to serve each month, was reduced to thirty-six.[28]

In 1919 Stamfordham wrote to the then Clerk, Hubert Burge,[29] making a further change: 'There will in future be no Chaplains in Ordinary; nor Honorary Chaplains. They will all be "Chaplains to the King". The future Clerk and Deputy Clerk will receive a salary of £50, and the chaplains now in receipt of £30 will be paid no salary, but the sum of five guineas will be paid each time they are summoned to preach.' The Clerk of the Closet remained as head of the college, charged to suggest the names of possible new royal chaplains: 'I do trust,' Stamfordham wrote to Burge in December 1922, 'that you will continue to recommend to the King men who are likely to move on to higher places, and thus keep up the healthy flow of new blood which has been secured during the last ten years.' So also began the healthy flow of correspondence between Clerk and Private Secretary on the subject of appointments.

Stamfordham took enormous trouble over the new appointments: 'Please consider about the vacancy,' is a typical communication to the Clerk, 'as I know I shall be bombarded with applications especially from the Royal Family at Kensington in favour of —— but I think we can do better than him. How would —— do? One hears that he is doing very good work in ——, or perhaps you think we ought to have a scholar; but please also a preacher.' There are many letters in that vein, bringing out the fact that the position which gradually became established during the 1930s whereby practically all the nominations came from the Clerk was then far from everyone's mind. Nominations then came down from the Crown; only very rarely did they come up from the Clerk, as is almost entirely the case now.

With that close personal involvement there sometimes came the need for censure: the King was 'very concerned' that the great Woodbine Willy [Studdert-Kennedy] preached in St Martin-in-the-Fields on Armistice Day 1922, only its third anniversary, that 'our claim to be fighting for honour and liberty was all pretence' and that he was ashamed of the part he played in encouraging men. 'If Studdert-Kennedy feels like that,' wrote Stamfordham to Burge, 'the King wonders how he can reconcile his position with strict loyalty to His Majesty who has selected him as one of his own chaplains. Why too does he not give up his Military Cross? It might of course be better to leave the matter alone, but in the event of any communication being made in the king's name, it should I feel come from you as head of the College of Chaplains.' There is, however, no record of any rebuke being administered to this idol of the British public, who drew such crowds wherever he went.

Not long after that event, the rector of Sandringham applied for a chaplaincy for the head of the Industrial Christian Fellowship, partly on the grounds that it would be a good move with Labour. 'But personally,' wrote Stamfordham, 'I should hardly have thought the man was up to our standard.' He was not nominated. The King himself during those years preferred men who had done well in the War: 'Archdeacon —— got an MC and Bar and was most popular as senior chaplain in the Guards' was a clear recommendation. On the other side of the coin, a chaplain who was arrested on a charge of 'interfering with people in the Park' received at Stamfordham's suggestion a letter from the Clerk asking ('painful as it is to me to write this') for his resignation. The chaplain in question wrote a long screed back, protesting his innocence and explaining that there was to be an appeal. Evidently this was successful, as he was still a chaplain four years later; but some time afterwards, when changes were being made in the College, this man was not offered an honorary chaplaincy 'because of that incident in the Park some time back'.

Once Stamfordham was caught out ('I had no idea Armstrong Hill was dead'), but usually the correspondence shows continued care: 'I should like to get someone from the Northern Province . . .'; or 'we might take a good typical parish priest this time'. To a rare suggestion from the Clerk of a particular priest came the reply: 'I must candidly admit that I have experienced indications of an apparent peevishness and may I say huffiness of disposition, and I should hesitate to advise HM to nominate him.' 'I must confess,' mused Stamfordham in June 1920, 'I often have disagreeable heart questionings whether the Chapel Royal justifies its existence, both from the point of view that the King never goes there, and from that of the Church. If only the public could be sure of hearing a good sermon, the Chapel would be filled instead of almost empty as it is now unless a well-known preacher is announced.' But when a good sermon was preached, Stamfordham noted the fact: '30 May 1924. Herbert of St George's, Camberwell, preached here [Buckingham Palace] this morning. The only criticism of his sermon was that it was too short. The King was much pleased, and also with his chat with Herbert after the service, and said to me: "We must keep an eye on him." He was your recommendation – please give us some more.' Herbert, of course, was that Percy Mark Herbert who was himself to be Clerk of the Closet eighteen years later. It is curious, incidentally, that no such letters as these between Stamfordham and Burge survive from Boyd Carpenter's time despite the latter's evident concern for the formation of the College of Chaplains.

A similar bond existed when Thomas Strong[30] was Clerk and Lord Wigram was Private Secretary. In 1933 Wigram wrote to Strong: 'You know the type of man His Majesty wants for his chaplains – youngish, likely to be promoted, a good preacher, and a pleasant personality to invite to preach at Sandringham and stay for the week-end. With regard to having some chaplains holding Anglo-Catholic views I do not think this signifies, tho' of course it would not do to select men who are in direct opposition to their bishop, or on the verge of joining the Roman Church. For instance the Bishop of St Albans [Furse] whom I have always regarded as being on the 'High Side' is a great friend of their Majesties and has stayed and preached at Sandringham twice this year, while the Bishop of Truro [Frere] has more than once preached at Buckingham Palace.'

In the twenties and thirties the cathedrals of the Old Foundation (i.e. those founded before the Reformation) were deemed superior to those founded in the sixteenth century, and the provosts of the newest cathedrals, such as Sheffield or Portsmouth, were seen to be in a different category from deans. In May 1932 Wigram wrote from Windsor to the Clerk: 'The Archbp. of C. was here for the weekend so I discussed with him the question of Provosts remaining Chaplains to the King [after their preferment]. He entirely agreed with us that they should be allowed to do so. We decided that they were more like Archdeacons. Deans are appointed by the PM and approved by the King; in most cases they become Provosts because the particular church they are attached to is made a Cathedral Church'. That ruling, long since forgotten, would not be popular with the present Annual Conference of Deans and Provosts. Another ruling, dating from February 1935, has also been overturned: 'the King is inclined to think, following the B[ishop] of Fulham's letter, that perhaps one appointment among HM Chaplains might be reserved for an English priest serving abroad.' The same notion, to appoint a Chaplain from the Diocese of Europe, was not proceeded with in the 1980s, but The Queen decided in 1986 to keep in the College of Chaplains the rector of Sandringham when he became the parish priest of the Falkland Islands, perhaps as a special case.

In 1964, after a good deal of correspondence, it was agreed that seventy should be the retirement age for Chaplains; but the rule was not made retrospective, and five years later five octogenarians were still in office. The Clerk wrote to them suggesting that two might remain and be appointed Extra Chaplains: 'Tubby' Clayton of Toc H fame, on account of his 'contribution to the life of the nation and of Society', and Selwyn Bean, formerly Archdeacon of Manchester and Prolocutor of the Church Assembly, for his 'contribution within the Church of England'. 'Tubby' Clayton wrote a characteristically rumbustious letter in reply to one from the Clerk:

'My dear Lord Bishop: I owe you a true debt for your personal note – a more than thoughtful act upon your part. The formal letter brings me no distress since I am more than conscious of my age and fully understand the situation. Some years before this honour was conferred by the grandfather of Her Majesty, when dear Dick Sheppard's father was I think Domestic Chaplain at Buckingham Palace, I well remember trembling when I came to preach therein; until by great good luck I found an old friend in a royal footman, who happened at that time to be on duty. I then was warned by the Domestic Chaplain that if he coughed I was to stop at once. Thus, after I had climbed into the pulpit and given my text and opening paragraph, the dear Domestic Chaplain started coughing. I therefore ceased and climbed down from the pulpit to the astonishment of all concerned, and no doubt to their immense relief. Her Majesty's grandfather then remarked, as he shook my hand, that my sermon was like a telegram not a speech. I ventured to explain why, when I was kindly told that Canon Sheppard was coughing more than usual on that day. Thus I escaped censure on all sides. At Sandringham there was no Canon Sheppard. Thus everything was happily arranged without his coughing habits interrupting . . . I am at 83 not overcome by sadness to resign the privilege of being on the Roll of Royal Chaplains, and am thankful to remain as Extra Chaplain . . . .' [31]

Today Extra Chaplains are still recommended by the Clerk when they would otherwise leave the College at the age of 70, and Her Majesty decides who should be specially honoured in this way.

Appointments to the College remain an important concern of the Clerk of the Closet, and it is his duty to keep it up to strength – or, rather, one under strength, as The Queen likes to keep the last place for an appointment entirely of her own choosing. The patronage of the other places lies initially with the Clerk. He keeps his ear to the ground, consults with bishops, gets second and third opinions on likely men, and then as vacancies occur submits a name or names to The Queen's Private Secretary for Her Majesty's approval. For each man he recommends he produces a paragraph on why he considers this particular priest suitable. If the message comes back, as it almost certainly will, that The Queen does too, the Clerk approaches the priest concerned to see if he would accept if the offer was made to him. (Some years ago an industrial chaplain refused on the grounds that it might have compromised his growing links with the shop floor). The formal invitation then follows from the Lord Chamberlain, and The Queen meets her new chaplain, and his wife and children, for the first time on the Terrace at a Buckingham Palace Garden Party in the July following. Chaplains are introduced to Her Majesty immediately after the National Anthem has been played and before The Queen goes down on the lawns.

This contact with The Queen is an innovation of the 1960s when Roger Wilson was Clerk in order to make sure that the Sovereign meets the priests he or she has appointed to the Household. Until the 1930s chaplains preached regularly in Buckingham Palace Chapel, but it was bombed in 1941 and not rebuilt, and the present chapel is on a much smaller scale, with seating for only fifteen or twenty people. Regular weekday celebrations of Holy Communion are held, but the royal chaplains do not preach there. In fact the Sovereign does not hear her chaplains preach in the Chapel Royal or the Queen's Chapel. Her Majesty's domestic chaplains at Sandringham and in the Great Park at Windsor are generally in the College, so the latter would certainly be the Chaplains to The Queen most 'sat under' by the Supreme Governor of the Church of England.

This distance between the sovereign and her chaplains naturally explains the change in the personal concern of the Sovereign over their appointment. The Clerk's responsibility takes a surprising amount of time. There are usually three or four vacancies each year – chaplains resign from the College on reaching the age of seventy or when they are appointed to a bishopric or deanery – but there is a fairly rapid turnover, and only five members in 1989 were members ten years earlier. The present members of the College range from the Chaplain-General of the Prison Service to a black West-Country vicar, from a non-stipendiary priest who practises as a lawyer in the Midlands to three former rectors of Sandringham and a theologian who specialises in ecumenical affairs for the Anglican communion. The age range is from forty to sixty-nine and the geographical spread from Berwick-on-Tweed to the Quantocks and the South Coast. The Clerk's writ does not, of course, extend to Wales, where the Church is not Established; nor to Scotland, where royal chaplains, from the Church of Scotland, come under the Dean of the Chapel Royal in Scotland.

In the 1980s The Queen's chaplains have met together on a number of social occasions, and thereby have much increased their feelings of collegiality. An invitation to them and their wives to the Palace at Wells for lunch and Cathedral Evensong in 1980 was followed by further gatherings in 1983, 1986 and 1989. In 1983 The Queen graciously invited the College to Windsor Castle, and herself came with Prince Philip to an act of worship in Windsor Parish Church where, as it happened, Her Majesty had not been to a church service for twenty-three years. In 1986 there was Evensong in Hatfield House Chapel, after a private tour of the house, by the kind invitation of the Marquess of Salisbury, and dinner together later in the Banqueting Hall, with a cheerful post-prandial performance by the doctors' group 'Instant Sunshine'. In 1989 The Queen asked the College with the Medical Household for the first time, to tea in Buckingham Palace with herself and Prince Philip, followed by Evensong in The Queen's Chapel and a reception at St James's Palace. These occasions are immensely appreciated, and undoubtedly give the chaplains a real feeling of belonging together within the Royal Household.

An amusing extra meeting for the College of Chaplains took place in 1985 when a national tabloid decided to 'do a feature' about the holder of the unlikely title of Clerk of the Closet, and the body of chaplains for which he was responsible. 'We'll pay for you all to meet,' said the newspaper, so we did, with a cheerful party in Westminster thrown in, and a photograph for good measure. The Dean very kindly allowed us to foregather in front of the cameras inside the Abbey after its doors had been closed to the public. The particular photographer the paper sent along much preferred his subjects to say 'whisky' rather than 'cheese' to achieve a smile, and to say it rather loudly at that. The Clerk, for one, was glad that the Abbey doors were firmly shut while thirty-six members of the Queen's Ecclesiastical Household were within declaiming 'whisky' fortissimo.

There was a nice Gilbertian interlude early in 1980 on the subject of scarlet cassocks. In March of that year The Queen visited a cathedral where the Greater Chapter, that is the Dean and residentiary canons, were in scarlet cassocks. Her Majesty was surprised, as she had always believed that this was the prerogative of Royal Chaplains and Royal Foundations, and she was not aware that this particular cathedral had any royal connections. So, on enquiry, it proved; for more than fifty years scarlet had been worn there just because they liked the colour!

The Clerk of the Closet was called upon to investigate the matter more widely. 'I have been asked by the Lord Chamberlain's Office to establish the fact that your cathedral clergy do not wear scarlet (i.e. Royal livery) cassocks! I apologise for bothering you with a matter which, however answered, will hardly bring in the Kingdom, but I want to help the Crown to get the countrywide pattern . . .'. That letter to forty-three cathedrals, dated 26 February 1982, revealed the undeniable truth that four cathedrals who were totally unauthorised to do so were wearing scarlet. They became embarrassed or irritated or rather angry when informed that they must desist; but a possibly explosive situation was averted by the Sovereign offering to pay for the Dean and three canons to move into some other coloured cassocks, as she was anxious they should not incur expense in the matter.

This typically generous gesture by The Queen was a quick emollient as far as the cathedrals were concerned. The Honorary Chaplains to the Forces, where there is an establishment of three or four men entitled at any one time to wear scarlet, were less amenable to being informed that on resigning from their respective services they should (unless Chaplain of the Fleet, Chaplain-General or Chaplain in Chief) surrender their scarlet and return to wearing black cassocks. This ruling was made because it was discovered that something in the region of 530 men up and down the country, all former chaplains in the services, were continuing to wear their scarlet after retirement (aged fifty-five) as against a mere twenty who had been Chaplains to the Queen. Unhappy about it or not, the service chaplains' acceptance of the new plan means that priests wearing the scarlet cassock will be more honoured rather than less because of their rarity. Hundreds of choirs have, long since, adopted scarlet, so the ecclesiastical tailors will be able to go on using their stock of cloth, since the Lord

Chamberlain decided it would be an unequal struggle to try and get them all out of the Royal livery, although he issued a statement to say he hoped choirs and servers would 'gradually phase out' its use. A reasonable attempt, therefore, full of the Englishman's gift for compromise, was made to regularise arrangements which had only begun seventy years before when King Edward VII first put his Chaplains-in-Ordinary in scarlet.

NOTES

1. B.L. Add. MS. 21480, 59899; P.R.O., E 36/214; *Bulletin John Rylands Library* xliii (1960), 40.
2. *LP* v, 309, 314, 321, 756, 761; xiii(2), 526, 529; xiv(2), 306; xxi(1), 67; P.R.O., E 36/232; B.L. Eg. MS. 2604, f. 6; Nicolas, N.H. (ed.), *Privy Purse Expenses of Henry VIII, 1529–32*, (1827), 174, 282.
3. Myers, *Household of Edward IV*, 137.
4. Emden, A.B., *Biographical Register of the University of Oxford*, passim.
5. *LP* i(1), 14; P.R.O., LC 2/1, f. 125; Emden, *Biographical Register*, passim.
6. *LP* iii(1), 242; Russell, J.G., *The Field of Cloth of Gold* (1969), 195.
7. *LP* xii(2), 319.
8. Ibid., xvi, 202.
9. P.R.O., LC 2/2, f. 38; Emden, *Biographical Register*, passim.
10. P.R.O., LC 2/3, pp. 97, 120; 2/3/2, p. 52; Harvey, J.H., *Early Nurserymen* (1974), 28.
11. P.R.O., LC 2/4/1, fos. 18v., 20.
12. *Acts of Privy Council*, iv. 148; Collinson, P., *Archbishop Grindal* (1979), 60.
13. P.R.O., LC 2/4/1, fos. 17–18; 2/4/2, fos. 28v.–29v.; 2/4/3, fos. 97–8.
14. Ibid., LC 2/4/4, fos. 54–55v.
15. Ibid., LC 2/4/6, fos. 29v., 42v.
16. Ibid., LC 2/5, fos. 36v.–37.
17. Ibid., fos. 44v.–45.
18. Ibid., LC 2/6, fos. 40v.–42v.
19. Ibid., LC 3/1.
20. Ibid., LC 3/3.
21. *Collections of Ordinances* (1790), 359.
22. *The Present State of the British Court* (1720), 48–9.
23. *Royal Kalendar* (1807).
24. Ibid., (1806, 1810).
25. Information from Mr David Baldwin, Sergeant of the Vestry, quoting the Cheque Book of the Chapel Royal, 229; *Clergy List* (1864).
26. Crockford, *Clerical Directory* (1894).
27. H.D.A. Major, *The Life and Letters of William Boyd Carpenter* (1925).
28. Windsor Castle, Royal Archives, Geo. V. 1.70/15.
29. Oxford, County Record Office, Burge Papers.
30. Ibid., Strong Papers.
31. Personal papers of Bishop Roger Wilson.

EPILOGUE: CLOSE TO THE SOVEREIGN

WHEN JOHN DOLBEN was Clerk of the Closet to Charles II it was said that he became so familiar with the King as on occasion to play with His Majesty's band-strings. Nathaniel Crew, Dolben's successor but one, so his biographer declares, 'behaved always with the exact courtesy of a gentleman.' A Bible and two Prayer Books with the royal monogram from the Chapel Royal, one of each now displayed at Auckland Castle, are tangible proofs of the King's personal links with his aristocratic Clerk.[1] At the very end of the century, in William III's reign, the Clerk was described as being 'commonly a Reverend, Sober and Learned Divine. His office is to resolve all doubts concerning Spiritual Matters, and to wait on His Majesty in His Closet or Private Oratory.'[2] The personal relationship of Clerk and Sovereign was very close. In his younger days, first as Tutor to two of the Royal Princes and later as Clerk, Richard Hurd was very close to his King, and letters between them either marking royal birthdays or accompanying gifts, often included personal remarks which bespoke the intimate relationship of former times.[3]

Dolben, Crew and Hurd were three among many Clerks whom surviving sources reveal to have been there to offer the Sovereign advice, support or friendship of a special kind. In turn, Sovereigns have, in different ways, rewarded their Clerks for a duty which all, so far as such information survives, have seen as an honour and a privilege. For several holders of the office the Clerkship led to greater responsibilities and rewards: for several under the Stuart Kings a bishopric; for later Clerks promotion to a wealthier see or to the Primacy of York or Canterbury. For many in more modern times it was reward enough to be able to serve and befriend the Sovereign and the Royal Family. The three most recent Clerks to retire from office have each received a knighthood in the Royal Victorian Order, that order of chivalry which it is the Sovereign's choice alone to bestow.

Over more than five centuries the office of Clerk of the Closet has changed in character, but many of the fifty-five holders since 1437 have, in a variety of ways, exercised important influence at the heart of the Royal Household in a post obscure to many, unknown to most, and until now something of a mystery even to those familiar with the Clerk and his duties in the late twentieth century.

NOTES

1. Whiting, C.E., *Nathaniel Lord Crewe, Bishop of Durham (1674–1721) and his Diocese* (Church Historical Soc. 1940), 24, 82–3.
2. Miege, G., *The Present State of Great Britain* (1691), 174.
3. Fortescue, J., (ed.), *The Correspondence of King George III (1760–83)*, (1928), vi. 87, 103–5, 115–16, 375–6, 441–2; Aspinall, A., (ed.), *The Later Correspondence of George III*, (1962), i. 113, 183, 194, 242–3, 380, 584; ii. 634; iii. 284, 293, 309n–10, 335, 360, 549, 619; iv. 143, 185, 331.

APPENDICES

APPENDIX 1:
CLERKS OF THE CLOSET
1437–1989

EDWARD ATHERTON
Died 1457

by 18 Mar. 1437 (*Cal. Pat.* 1436–41, 17)

WILLIAM SAVAGE

by Mich. 1466, still Mich. 1467
(P.R.O., E 101/412/2, f. 37)

ALEXANDER LEIGH
Almoner by 1474; alive 1503

by Mich. 1466, still Mich. 1467 (Ibid.)

PETER GREVES

by Feb. 1503; until 1509 (P.R.O., LC
2/1, f. 67v.; *LP* i(1) 40–1, 204)

GEOFFREY WRENNE
Canon of Windsor 1514, died
1527

by 5 Dec. 1509, still 16 Nov. 1514 (*LP*
i(1) 128, i(2) 1446)

RICHARD RAWSON
Canon of Windsor 1523, died
1543

by Mich. 1525, to ? 1529 (*LP* iv 748, v
307)

THOMAS WESTBY
Archdeacon of York 1540, died
about 1544

? from 1529, still 1534 (*LP* v 309, 314,
748, vii 345)

GEORGE WOLFETT
Canon of Salisbury 1531, died
1554

by 3 Feb. 1537, to Mich. 1538 (*LP* xi(1)
148, xiii(2) 535)

EDWARD LEIGHTON or
LAUGHTON
Archdeacon of Salisbury 1539,
died 1551

Mich. 1538 to Mich. 1544 (*LP* xiii(2)
535, xix(2) 309, xx(1) 184)

JOHN RUDDE
  Preb. Durham 1550, Winchester
  1551, died 1578

Mich. 1544, still 1547, ? still 1553 (*LP*
xx(1) 184; P.R.O., LC 2/2 f. 38, 2/4/1 f.
20)

JOHN RICARDE
  Died by 10 Nov. 1558

by 26 Dec. 1556 (*Cal. Pat.* 1555–7, 254)

THOMAS THURLANDE
  Master of the Savoy 1559, died
  1574

by 17 Nov. 1558 (P.R.O., LC 2/4/2,
f. 28v.)

WILLIAM YONGE
  Preb. of Westminster 1560, died
  by 1579

by 15 Jan. 1559 (P.R.O., LC 2/4/3,
p. 108)

WILLIAM ABSOLON
  Master of the Savoy 1576, died
  1586

by 10 Aug. 1576; still 1 Jan. 1579 (*Cal.
Pat.* 1575–8, 74; *Progresses and Public
Processions of Queen Eliz.*, ed. J. Nichols,
ii 260, 271)

JOHN THORNBOROUGH
  Bp of Limerick 1593, of Bristol
  1603, of Worcester 1617, died
  1641

by 1 Jan. 1589, still Mar. 1603
(*Progresses*, iii 10, 19; P.R.O., LC 2/4/4,
f. 54)

RICHARD NEILE
  Dean of Westminster 1605, Bp
  of Rochester 1608, of Coventry
  and Lichfield 1610, of Lincoln
  1614, of Durham 1617, of
  Winchester 1628; Archbp of
  York 1632, died 1640

Sworn 26 July 1603 (P.R.O. LS13/168,
p. 91)

[JOHN BUCKERIDGE
  Bp of Rochester; Bp of Ely
  1628, died 1631]

Said, in error, to have been appointed
by 21 June 1617 (*Cal. S.P. Dom.*
1611–18, 473)

WILLIAM JUXON
  Dean of Worcester; Bp elect of
  Hereford 1633; Bp of London
  1633, Archbp of Canterbury
  1660, died 1663

sworn 10 July 1632, until ? Aug. 1633
(*D.N.B.* based on Laud's Diary)

MATTHEW WREN
  Bp of Hereford 1634, of
  Norwich 1635; Dean of Chapel
  Royal 1636, Bp of Ely 1638,
  died 1667

appted 20 Oct. 1633; until ? 1636
(*D.N.B.* based on Stephen Wren,
Parentalia)

RICHARD STEWARD
  Dean of Chichester; Dean of
  Westminster 1645; died 1651

by 20 Jan. 1638 (*Cal. S.P. Dom.* 1637–8,
173)

GILBERT SHELDON
Dean of Chapel Royal 1660; Bp
of London 1660; Archbp of
Canterbury 1663; died 1677

c. 1646 (Anthony Wood, *Athenae
Oxonienses*, iv. 854)

JOHN EARLE
Dean of Westminster; Bp of
Worcester 1662, of Salisbury
1663, died 1665

sworn 9 June 1660 (P.R.O. LC 3/24)

JOHN DOLBEN
Dean of Westminster; Bp of
Rochester 1666; Almoner by
1675; Archbp of York 1683, died
1686

sworn 15 June 1664 (Ibid.)

WALTER BLANDFORD
Bp of Oxford; Bp of Worcester
1671, died 1675

sworn 7 Feb. 1667 (Ibid.)

NATHANIEL CREW
Dean of Chichester; Bp of
Oxford 1671, Bp of Durham
1674; died 1721

sworn 6 Apr. 1669, 14 Mar. 1685
(P.R.O., LC 3/24. 26, 56)

THOMAS SPRAT
Bp of Rochester; died 1713

29 Dec. 1685 (Hist. MSS. Com.
Downshire MSS., 1(i), 83)

GILBERT BURNET
Bp of Salisbury 1689, died 1715

by 14 Feb. 1689 (*Cal. S.P. Dom.*
1689–90, 1)

JOHN TILLOTSON
Dean of St Paul's, 1689
Archbp of Canterbury 1691,
died 1694

by 22 Apr. 1691 (*Cal. S.P. Dom.*
1690–1, 342)

THOMAS BURNETT
Master of Charterhouse; died
1715

admitted 28 Nov., sworn 7 Dec. 1691
(P.R.O., LC 3/31–2, LC 13/198, p. 65;
Cal. S.P. Dom, 1691–2, 20)

JOHN MONTAGU
Master of Trinity, Cambridge;
Dean of Durham 1699, died 1723

sworn 25 Nov. 1695 (P.R.O., LC 3/3, 31;
LS 13/198, p. 78)

JOHN YOUNGER
Dean of Salisbury 1705, died
1728

WILLIAM GRAHAM
Dean of Carlisle; Dean of Wells
1704, died 1713

sworn to attend 1 Apr. 1702; sworn as
Clerk 26 Nov. 1702 (P.R.O. LS 13/43
LC 5/161, p. 100, LC 5/166)

SAMUEL PRATT
Master of the Savoy; Dean of
Rochester 1706, died 1723

CHARLES TRIMNELL
Bp of Norwich; Bp of
Winchester 1721, died 1723

between 11 Apr. and 28 May 1715
(*Diaries of Wm. Nicolson*, 618, 622)

RICHARD WILLIS
Bp of Salisbury; Almoner; Bp of
Winchester 1723; died 1734

sworn 7 Nov. 1723, 3 Oct. 1727
(P.R.O., LC 3/64; LS 13/200, p. 66)

HENRY EGERTON
Bp of Hereford; died 1746

sworn 12 Mar. 1735 (P.R.O., LC 3/65,
p. 30)

JOSEPH BUTLER
Bp of Bristol; Bp of Durham
1750; died 1752

sworn 17 Apr. 1746, 6 Apr. 1749
(P.R.O. LC 3/65, p. 197; 3/18, p. 9)

JOHN GILBERT
Bp of Salisbury; Archbp of York
1757; died 1761

sworn 22 Nov. 1752 (P.R.O. LC 3/65,
p. 262)

JOHN THOMAS
Bp of Salisbury; Bp of
Winchester 1761; died 1781

sworn 27 June 1757, 12 Dec. 1760
(P.R.O. LC 3/66, p. 32; 3/67, p. 22)

RICHARD HURD
Bp of Lichfield and Coventry;
Bp of Worcester 1781; died 1808

sworn 10 May 1781 (P.R.O. LC 3/67,
p. 125)

WILLIAM JACKSON
Bp of Oxford; died 1815

1813 (*Royal Kalendar*)

GEORGE PELHAM
Bp of Exeter; Bp of Lincoln
1820; died 1827

sworn 20 Dec. 1815 (P.R.O., LC 3/68,
p. 173)

ROBERT JAMES CARR
Bp of Chichester; Bp of
Worcester 1831; died 1841

sworn 8 Feb. 1827 (P.R.O., LC 3/69, p.
108)

EDWARD STANLEY
Bp of Norwich; died 1849

gazetted 17 July 1837 (*London Gaz.* p.
1832)

JOHN GRAHAM
Bp of Chester; died 1865

gazetted 25 Sept. 1849 (Ibid. p. 2977)

HENRY PHILPOTT
Bp of Worcester; died 1892

gazetted 27 June 1865 (*Annual Register*,
new series, 297)

RANDALL THOMAS
DAVIDSON
Bp of Rochester; Bp of
Winchester 1895; KCVO 1902;
Archbp of Canterbury 1903;
died 1930

gazetted 28 Apr. 1891 (*London Gaz.* p.
2302)

WILLIAM BOYD CARPENTER
Bp of Ripon; died 1918

27 Feb 1903 (*Lord Chamberlain's Annual Rep. 1903*)

HUBERT MURRAY BURGE
Bp of Oxford; died 1925

15 Nov. 1918 (*Lord Chamberlain's Annual Rep. 1918*)

THOMAS BANKS STRONG
Bp of Oxford; GBE 1918; died 1944

3 Nov. 1925 (*Lord Chamberlain's Annual Rep. 1925*)

CYRIL FORSTER GARBETT
Bp of Winchester; Archbp of York 1942; GCVO 1955; died 1955

30 Sept. 1937 (Windsor, Royal Archives, Geo VI 2543)

PERCY MARK HERBERT
Bp of Blackburn; Bp of Norwich 1942; KCVO 1954; died 1968

22 May 1942 (*Lord Chamberlain's Annual Rep. 1942*)

ROGER PLUMPTON WILSON
Bp of Chichester; KCVO 1974

1 Feb. 1963 (Lord Chamberlain's office, Warrant of Appointment bk.)

WILLIAM GORDON FALLOWS
Bp of Sheffield; died 1979

31 Oct. 1975 (Ibid.)

JOHN MONIER BICKERSTETH
Bp of Bath and Wells; KCVO 1989

1 Dec. 1979 (Warrant of Appointment)

JOHN WAINE
Bp of Chelmsford

6 Sept. 1989 (Lord Chamberlain's office, Warrant of Appointment bk.)

APPENDIX 2: CLERKS TO QUEENS CONSORT, PRINCES AND PRINCESSES

JOHN SWAN, Katherine of Aragon, 1509 — P.R.O., LC 9/50, f. 209v

THOMAS PEKEFALL, Prince Henry, 1511 — P.R.O., LC 2/1, f. 172v

HENRY ROWTE, Princess Mary, 1516–21 — P.R.O., E 36/232; *LP* ii(2), 1473

MR BARTON or BURTON, Prince Henry, 1612 — P.R.O., LC 2/4/6, f. 42v

THOMAS PATTEN, Queen Anne, 1619 — P.R.O., LC 2/5, f. 37

WILLIAM STANLEY, Queen Mary, 1689 — *Cal. S.P. Dom.* 1689–90, 1

JOSEPH BUTLER, Queen Caroline, 1737 — *D.N.B.*

FRANCIS AYSCOUGH, Prince of Wales, 1746–1750 — *Court and City Register*

STEPHEN HALES, Princess Dowager, 1752–61 — Ibid.

EDWARD YOUNG, Princess Dowager, 1761–65 — *D.N.B.; Court and City Register*

SAMUEL SQUIRE, Prince of Wales, 1757–60 — *Court and City Register*

CUTTS BARTON, Dowager Princess of Wales, 1766–72 — Ibid.

JOHN LOCKMAN, Prince of Wales, 1788–1807 — Ibid.; *New Annual Register* (1808)

FREDERICK WILLIAM BLOMBERG, Prince of Wales, 1808–20 — Ibid.

APPENDIX 3: DEPUTY CLERKS OF THE CLOSET

T HE PRACTICE OF appointing Deputy Clerks had arisen by the middle of the seventeenth century when in 1667 Nathaniel Crew, only recently made a Chaplain in Ordinary, became Deputy Clerk to Walter Blandford on the latter's nomination as Clerk.[1] It is not certain who made the appointment, nor why. By 1720 it was evidently standard practice to have Under Clerks, and Mr Egerton, probably Henry Egerton, himself a future Clerk, and Mr Talbot were appointed to serve 'by turns', by the then Clerk, Charles Trimnell.[2] Three Deputy Clerks had been appointed by 1746, during the Clerkship of Joseph Butler[3] and thereafter Deputies were a permanent part of the establishment, and clearly essential by the time Richard Hurd had become quite unable to leave Hartlebury. Henry William Majendie, tutor to Prince William, was clearly an admirable substitute for Hurd in the 1790s, and on his appointment as Bishop of Chester in 1800 Hurd was glad to write to the King nominating Charles Moss in his place 'in the absence of your disabled Clerk'.[4] Then or a little later the three Deputies, all unpaid, were Dr Charles Poyntz, John Fisher, and Moss; in 1803 Fisher was succeeded by the Hon. Dr Edward Legge; and by 1805 Dr William Cookson had been added to the number.[5]

The establishment of three Deputy Clerks continued throughout the nineteenth century. In 1874 the Prime Minister, Mr Disraeli, informed the Queen that the then Deputy Clerk of the Closet at St James's, the Hon. and Revd Edward Keppel, had resigned. There may, by this time, have been a slight change in the establishment, for Keppel's title seems to have combined the post of Deputy Clerk with that of 'Chaplain at St James's Palace' which had been part of the establishment in 1848. The salary, as Disraeli told the Queen, was £120 per annum, and 'as the post is one so near to Y[ou]r Majesty's person, Mr Disraeli ventures to think Y[ou]r Majesty might be disposed to make the selection yourself.'

Either on this vacancy or another about the same time Dean Wellesley of

Windsor wrote to the Queen as to 'the preference of Mr Duckworth to Dr Bradley for the present occasion. Your Majesty is aware that you have at present a Deputy Clerkship and a Chaplaincy to give away, with which you might gratify any of those distinguished men recommended by the Dean, only none should have both at once. If Your Majesty wishes to please both Sir T. Bidulph and Col Maude, you might give one of these to Mr Maude for the latter's brother. He is Rector of Great Munden, a quiet good kind man. As he is no preacher, the former office would be the best . . ..' Two days later Wellesley again wrote to the Queen: 'All Mr d'Israeli's letters confirm that he will never willingly propose to Your Majesty for high preference a clergyman of the Liberal Party. He regards the Church as a great state-engine of the Conservatives, and that any appointments with a tendency to its further reformation will weaken him politically with his party . . . he is shrewd enough to see that names may be supplied to you by clergymen with views his party does not like. Dr Lightfoot is at this moment standing up against "the atheistic and materialistic tendencies" mentioned by Your Majesty. He is a foremost man, and seems to the Dean to be the one whom Your Majesty might make Deputy Clerk.' Lightfoot was duly appointed and wrote from Trinity College, Cambridge, on 13 February 1875 of his 'grateful acceptance of the office of Deputy Clerk of the Closet.'[7] Lightfoot presumably left office on his appointment as Bishop of Durham in 1879.

On 27 July 1882 the Lord Steward, Earl Sydney of Scadbury, informed the Queen of 'a vacancy in the office of Deputy Clerk of the Closet by the lamented death of Dean Stanley' and suggested Canon Pearson, a friend of the late Dean.[8] The next day he learned that the Queen 'entirely' approved, and Pearson joined Dr Vaughan, who had been appointed earlier in the year.

Soon after Henry Philpott resigned the see of Worcester in November 1890 Randall Davidson was appointed Assistant Clerk, an office created to cover the peculiar circumstances of the Bishop's wish to remain as Clerk although no longer a diocesan bishop and in poor health.[9] In fact the post was gazetted as 'A Clerk of the Closet',[10] a significant phrase harking back to the time when Queen Anne had appointed three men to share the post. Three Deputies still remained in office, but in 1894 a vacancy occurred in their ranks which allowed an important intervention. In a letter to the Queen's Private Secretary on 2 February 1894 Davidson, then sole Clerk of the Closet, wrote: 'I suppose the Queen will take a personal part in selecting the man. It is a post which has been held by very prominent men. If some equally prominent man is now desired again (and I think myself the dignity of the office should be maintained) the following would any of them be possible: The present Dean of Westminster, Canon Prothero, Hon. and Revd E. Carr Glyn, Canon Ainger, Canon Dalton. The office is now very much a sinecure as the Queen has directed me, as Clerk of the Closet, to attend whenever a bishop does homage. I do not think the Sub-Dean of the Chapels Royal would be a good man for the position.'

In the event Dr Farrar, Dean of Westminster, was appointed and Canon J.N. Dalton became a Deputy three years later; but for all his protestations about the dignity of the office Davidson had, in fact, put paid to the post in a letter written in his own hand to the Lord Chamberlain on 23 April 1895: 'Perhaps if any new difficulties arise I may have an opportunity when B[isho]p Percival [of Hereford] is summoned for his Homage (which should be as soon as convenient) as I hope to be able to attend as Clerk of the Closet. By the way, will you when you write to the Home Office to fix the homage day remind them that the Queen has *commanded* my attendance on these occasions and not a Deputy Clerk's. Last time they summoned Mr Jolley from Cheshire and he found he was not wanted and they did not summon me! Also you will give me such notice about the day as you can.'[11] Davidson thus having restored the Clerk to an active role within the Royal Household, firmly putting the Home Office in its place and reminding the Lord Chamberlain that he, too, was a servant of the Queen, it was only a matter of time before the office of Deputy was the sinecure he had declared it to be.

There were still in 1902 three Deputy Clerks, Dr Farrar, Canon Dalton, and the Revd W.R. Jolley, but King Edward VII did not appoint anyone to succeed the latter, rather to the then Clerk's regret, and by 1910 Dalton was the senior Deputy.[12] By 1923 Dalton was the only one to survive, and the post died with him in 1931.[13] Since that time the Sub-Deans of the Chapel Royal have served as Deputy Clerks, and have always been at hand to deputise for the Clerk at a Homage, as has happened once or twice through sickness in the past ten years. Today the Deputy Clerk's closest link with his principal is that, as has already been described, in his capacity as Sub-Dean of the Chapels Royal, he arranges the Rota of Waits for the Chapel Royal and the Queen's Chapel. He, therefore, of all the Domestic Chaplains, hears more sermons from Chaplains to The Queen than anyone else, so he is in the habit of reminding the Clerk to make sure that he includes preaching qualities in his recommendations to the Sovereign.

NOTES

1. Whiting, C.E., *Nathaniel Lord Crewe*, 23.
2. *The Present State of the British Court. . .* (1720), 48.
3. *Court and City Register* (1746).

4. Aspinall, A., (ed.), *The Later Correspondence of George III*, (1962), iii. 335.
5. Ibid., iv. 111, 186n.
6. Windsor, Royal Archives A 47/60.
7. Ibid., D/6/12.
8. Ibid., C68/61.
9. Ibid., Vic. D 13A/148, 153, 156.
10. *London Gazette*, 28 April 1891, p. 2302.
11. Windsor, Royal Archives, Vic. D 12/16A.
12. Ibid. Geo. V 1.70/3, 7–8, 10–11.
13. Crockford, *Clerical Directory* (1902, 1923, 1932); *Who Was Who* (1929–40), 326.

APPENDIX 4: THE CLERK OF THE CLOSET AND THE KING'S EVIL

THE TRADITION THAT the touch of the sovereign could heal the glandular disease known as scrofula or the 'King's Evil' dates back in England to the reign of Edward the Confessor, and in France to that of Robert II (996–1031). The custom of touching was practised in England by Henry I and Henry II in the twelfth century, and the Household Ordinances of York of 1323 mention that the custom was continued by Edward II, to whom victims were brought by 'the chaplain', probably the Chief Chaplain of the Household.[1] A rite was established by the time of Henry VII entitled 'The Ceremonies for the Healing of them that be diseased with the King's Evil'. In the ceremony the King was accompanied by a chaplain who heard the sovereign's confession and read the Gospel. Each sick person, accompanied by the Clerk of the Closet, then knelt before the King and the words 'They shall impose hands upon the sick' from the Gospel were repeated over every person as the King touched them.

A second version of the ceremony is in a volume once belonging to Queen Mary but evidently somewhat earlier in date, since the rubrics refer to the King. This required the Clerk not only to kneel beside each victim before the sovereign, but to accompany him or her from the royal presence, and an illustration of the ceremony shows the Clerk habited in cassock and gown, actually kneeling behind the sick person holding open the collar of the patient's coat.

Under Charles I the ceremony was slightly varied in that, after the touching was complete, a second Gospel was read and the Clerk of the Closet presented a gold coin or medal, known as a touch piece, on a white silk riband to the King for each patient. It is not surprising, in view of their claims to Divine Right, that the Stuart Kings appear to have encouraged the ceremony. Charles II touched no less than 90,798 people, and the Duke of Monmouth was popularly recognised as his rightful successor as a result of his own successful touchings in the 1680s. The rite as practised under Henry VII was printed in 1686 by command of James II, perhaps as a conscious attempt to emphasise that the ceremony predated the Reformation. James himself touched as many as 350 people at one time. Queen Anne was the last English sovereign to perform the ceremony, but touch pieces were issued by the Stuart Pretenders – the Old Pretender as James III and the Cardinal of York as Henry IX. Versions of the rite were printed in 1713, 1715, and 1727, but in none was the Clerk of the Closet given a specific role in the rubrics.[2] The 1686 version was reprinted, probably as a matter of antiquarian interest, in 1789.[3]

NOTES

1. T.F. Tout, *The Place of the Reign of Edward II in English History* (Manchester 1914), 317.
2. *Journal of the British Archaeological Association*, xxvii (1871), 282–307.
3. Lambeth Palace Library H5147.K5.

APPENDIX 5: THE CLERK'S BADGE OF OFFICE

IN 1906 KING Edward VII approved the replacement of the embroidered scarf hitherto worn by Chaplains in Ordinary by a metal badge. That same badge was also worn by successive Clerks until 1986 although Boyd Carpenter found himself in a difficulty in 1910 ('I don't want to be troublesome') because he could not accept the badge at the hands of his Deputy.[1]

Each Clerk until 1979 wore the badge pinned to the left hand side of his black scarf. From taking office in December of that year the new Clerk began wearing the badge on his cassock immediately below his clerical collar. This was with Her Majesty's own gracious agreement, the case for a new position having been made on the grounds that a bishop was not very often in convocation robes, and thus the scarf was seldom worn. The badge would not be in order on the priestly stole, much more often worn by a bishop either with eucharistic vestments or with cope and mitre. On the cassock, worn whenever a bishop was on duty, the badge would be clearly visible and would remain so whatever else the bishop might be wearing on top.

However, frequently re-pinning the badge into its place on the cassock proved neither good for the badge nor the cassock. This was a fact which the Lord Chamberlain must have recognised, for on the day of Her Majesty's sixtieth birthday celebrations, on 21 April 1986 just before the special service in St George's Chapel, Windsor, he produced, as a complete surprise, a specially designed and very handsome collar badge for the Clerk to wear during his period of office, just as in 1977 the Almoner had been presented with a badge of office for the first time.

The badge has now become the official emblem of the Clerk's office, for the Court Circular of 26 October 1989 read as follows: 'The Right

Reverend John Waine (Bishop of Chelmsford) had the honour of being received by Her Majesty upon his appointment as Clerk of the Closet to The Queen, and received his Badge of Office.'

NOTE

1. Windsor, Royal Archives, Geo. V I. 70/3, 6.

APPENDIX 6:
THE CLERK'S SALARY

T HE SALARY OF the Clerk of the Closet is clearly the most consistent feature of an office which has in all other respects changed in both status and influence in its long history. The Household Ordinance of 1478, recording two 'clerkes of the closettes', presumably one each for the sovereign and his consort, awarded each a wage of 4½d. a day and no other livery.[1] John Rudde in 1525–6 received £6 16s. 10½d., exactly the same salary with an extra day's pay for a leap year. The established salary for the two Clerks in Elizabeth's reign was £4 apiece; in 1606 it was £6 13s. 4d., in 1630–1 and 1689 £6 18s., and in 1699 £6 13s. 4d.[2] The salary was elsewhere expressed in 1691 at 20 nobles, and in 1720 at £6 18s., on the latter occasion with an allowance of £50 for surplices and other necessaries, and £3 5s. for providing table linen.[3]   In 1891 the Queen's Private Secretary thought that there were no emoluments attached to the office when he wrote asking whether Randall Davidson might serve as Assistant to the ageing Bishop Philpott, but he declared that the Clerk received a fee of £2 at each Homage.[4] The question of salary was raised early in King George V's reign: there was a suggestion that it be raised from £7 to £120, but Douglas Dawson, Comptroller at the Lord Chamberlain's Office, was rather more guarded, agreeing with Lord Stamfordham, the King's Private Secretary, that the Clerk should certainly have a salary, but noting that although he came under the jurisdiction of the Lord Chamberlain, the Lord Steward actually paid both him and the Chaplains.[5]

In September 1975 the Establishment Officer at Buckingham Palace declared himself 'intrigued' that the Clerk 'attracts an annual salary amounting to the princely sum of £7' and enquired of the Lord Chamberlain's Office how long such a sum had been paid and what it represented. A month later his correspondent admitted defeat. There the matter rests; the Homage fee has not been paid for years, but the Clerk still has the fun of receiving his princely sum from the Keeper of the Privy Purse, after tax deductions, in four quarterly instalments.

NOTES

1. Myers, *Household of Edward IV*, 225.
2. *A Collection of Ordinances and Regulations for the Government of the Royal Household* (Society of Antiquaries, 1790), 169, 250–1, 408; Peck, F., *Desiderata Curiosa*, ii. 8; 'Offices and Fees of the King's Household', *Archaeologia* xv (1806), 80; P.R.O., LS 13/30; Miege, G., *New State of Great Britain*.
3. Miege, G., *The New State of England* (1691), 174; *The Present State of the British Court* (1720), 48–9.
4. Windsor, Royal Archives, Vic. D13A/153.
5. Ibid. Royal Archives, Geo. V 1233/2.

SOURCES

British Library:

Additional MSS: 21480–1,   Household Books of Henry VII kept by John
Heron, 1499–1505, 1509–18
36056–7,   Hardwicke Papers
59899,   Chamber Issue and Memoranda Book, 1502–5

Egerton MSS: 1708, Egerton Family Papers

Public Record Office:

Exchequer:
E 36/214 John Heron's Account Book, 1505–9
   232 Wages of Royal Household, Henry VIII

E 101/407–15 Various Accounts, Wardrobe Accounts, 1421–1503

E 361/7–8 Enrolled accounts of Keeper of the Wardrobe, 1399–1553

Lord Chamberlain's Department:
LC 2/1–6 Royal Funerals and Mourning, 1500–1626

LC 3 Registers:
  /1   Establishment of the Household, 1641–44
   3   Establishment of the Household, 1695–99
   4   Establishment of the Household, 1700–02
 18   Establishment of the Household, 1749
 24   Rough Establishment Book, 1660 and Cheque Roll, 1660–84
 26   Rough Establishment Book, 1666
 31   Royal Establishment Book, 1626–97
 32   Royal Establishment Book, 1688–95
 33   Admissions to office, 1660–1748
 34   Admissions to office, 1837–50
 56   Appointment Book, series I, 1685
 64   Appointment Book, series I, 1724–33
 65   Appointment Book, series I, 1733–56
 66   Appointment Book, series I, 1755–60
 67   Appointment Book, series I, 1760–93

68 Appointment Book, series I, 1793–1820
69 Appointment Book, series I, 1820–30

LC 5 Miscellanea:
/65 Wardrobe, copies of warrants, provisions, 1676–80
161 Warrant Books, General, 1738–53
166 Warrant Books, Various, 1687–1714
237 Appointments, 1851–68
240 Appointments, 1890–98

LC 9/50 Accounts, Great Wardrobe, 1483–1509

Lord Steward's Department:
LS 13 Miscellaneous Books:
/30 Establishment, 1627
43 Establishment, 1702
168 Entry Book of Records
169 Entry Book of Records
198 Servants, Certificate Book of Admissions, 1689–1701
200 Servants, 1714–27

Windsor Castle, Royal Archives:

Correspondence
Queen Victoria's Journal

Oxford County Record Office:

Papers of Bishops Burge and Strong

BIBLIOGRAPHY

Annual Register, 1758–1862

Annual Register (New Series), 1863–1946

Anson, Harold, *T.B. Strong: Bishop, musician, Dean, Vice-chancellor*, 1949

Aspinall, A., (ed.), *The Later Correspondence of George III*, 1962

Bell, G.K.A., *Randall Davidson*, 3rd edn., 1952

Campbell, W., (ed.), *Materials for the Reign of Henry VII*, (Rolls series), 2 vols. 1873–7

Chadwick, O., *The Victorian Church*, 2 vols. 1966, 1970

Chamberlayne, E., *The Present State of England*, various editions

Charnwood, Lord, (ed.), *Discourses and Letters of Hubert Murray Burge*, with a Memoir (1930)

Chrimes, S.B., *Administrative History of Medieval England*, 1952

Clergy Lists

C[ockayne], G.E., *The Complete Peerage*, ed. V. Gibbs, H.A. Doubleday, etc., 14 vols., 1910–40

A Collection of Ordinances and Regulations for the Government of the Royal Household, Society of Antiquaries, 1790

Collinson, P., *Archbishop Grindal*, 1979

Colvin, H.M., (ed.), *History of the King's Works*, 6 vols., 1963–82

The Court and City Register, 1746

Crockford's Clerical Directory

Discourses and Letters of Hubert Murray Burge, ed. with a Memoir by Lord Charnwood, 1930

Emden, A.B., *Biographical Register of the University of Cambridge*

Emden, A.B., *Biographical Register of the University of Oxford to 1500*

Emden, A.B., *Biographical Register of the University of Oxford, 1501– 40*

Evelyn, J., *Diary*, ed. W. Bray, 4 vols. 1887.

Fortescue, J., (ed.), *Correspondence of King George III (1760–83)*, 1928

Foster, J., *Alumni Oxonienses, 1500–1714*, 4 vols. 1892

Harvey, J.H., *Gothic England*, 1948

Harvey, J.H., *Early Nurserymen*, 1974

Hennessy, G., *Novum Repertorium Ecclesiasticum Parochiale Londoniense*, 1898

Johnson, C., (ed.), *Dialogus de Scaccario*, 1950

Laud, W., *Diary*, in *Works*, 1847–60

Lord Chamberlain's Annual Reports

Lyte, Maxwell, (ed.), *The Registers of Bishops Wolsey, Clerke, Knyght and Bourne*, (Somerset Record Society lv)

Major, H.D.A., *The Life and Letters of William Boyd Carpenter*, 1925

Miege, G., *The New State of England, under their Majesties King William and Queen Mary*, 1691

Myers, A.R., *The Household of Edward IV: the Black Book and the Ordinance of 1478*, 1959

The New Annual Register, 1780–1821

Nichols, J., *The Progresses and Public Processions of Queen Elizabeth*, 3 vols. 1823

Nicolas, N.H., (ed.), *Privy Purse Expenses of Henry VIII, 1529–32*, 1827

Nicolas, N.H., (ed.), *Proceedings and Ordinances of the Privy Council of England*, 7 vols., 1834–7

Peck, F., *Desiderata Curiosa*, 2 vols., 1779

The Present State of the British Court, 1720

Rider, C., *Rider's British Merlin*, 1800

The Royal Kalendar of Complete and Correct Annual Register, 1808–13

Russell, J.G., *The Field of Cloth of Gold*, 1969

Strange, William, *Sketches of Her Majesty's Household*, 1848

Smyth, C., *Cyril Forster Garbett, Archbishop of York*, 1959

Somerville, R., *The Savoy: Manor, Hospital, Chapel*, 1960

Squibb, G.D., *Doctor's Commons*, 1977

Strype, J., *Annals of the Reformation*, 1824

Tout, T.F., *The Place of the Reign of Edward II in English History*, 1914

Venn, J. and J.A., *Alumni Cantabrigienses*, 2 parts, 10 vols. 1922–54

Weaver, F.W., (ed.), *Somerset Medieval Wills, 1531–58*, (Somerset Record Society xxi)

Whiting, C.E., *Nathaniel Lord Crewe, Bishop of Durham (1674–1721) and his Diocese 1940*

Wood, Anthony, *Athenae Oxonienses* ed. P.Bliss, 4 vols. 1813–20

Wraxall, N.W., *Historical Memoirs*, 1836

INDEX